Sweaters by Hand

Sweaters by Hand

Hélène Rush & Rachael Emmons

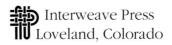 Interweave Press
Loveland, Colorado

Illustrations by Ann Sabin
Photography by Joe Coca
Supplementary black-and-white photography by
Bruce Emmons, Deborah Robson, and Diane Langley
Typesetting by Marc M. Owens
Cover design and photo styling by Ann Sabin

Special thanks to Gallery East for supplying
accessories, to Jeremiah and Susan Rohr for letting us
use their truck, and to The Farm at Lee Martinez
Park, in Fort Collins, Colorado, for permission to
hold a photography session at dawn.

INTERWEAVE PRESS
306 North Washington Avenue
Loveland, Colorado 80537

Library of Congress Catalog Number 88-32898
ISBN 0-934026-37-8
First printing:5M:1188:OB/CL

Library of Congress Cataloging-in-Publication Data
Rush, Hélène.
  Sweaters by hand.

  Bibliography: p.
  Includes index.
  Knitting—Patterns. 2. Sweaters. 3. Hand
spinning. I. Emmons, Rachael, 1944-   . II Title.
TT825.T94 1988   746.9'2   88-32898
ISBN 0-934026-37-8

Sweaters by Hand

Hélène Rush & Rachael Emmons

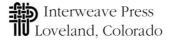 Interweave Press
Loveland, Colorado

Illustrations by Ann Sabin
Photography by Joe Coca
Supplementary black-and-white photography by
Bruce Emmons, Deborah Robson, and Diane Langley
Typesetting by Marc M. Owens
Cover design and photo styling by Ann Sabin

Special thanks to Gallery East for supplying
accessories, to Jeremiah and Susan Rohr for letting us
use their truck, and to The Farm at Lee Martinez
Park, in Fort Collins, Colorado, for permission to
hold a photography session at dawn.

 INTERWEAVE PRESS
306 North Washington Avenue
Loveland, Colorado 80537

Library of Congress Cataloging-in-Publication Data
Rush, Hélène.
  Sweaters by hand.

  Bibliography: p.
  Includes index.
  Knitting—Patterns. 2. Sweaters. 3. Hand
spinning. I. Emmons, Rachael, 1944-   . II Title.
TT825.T94 1988   746.9'2   88-32898
ISBN 0-934026-37-8

CONTENTS

Preface   **1**

A special note for non-spinners 1 / An introductory note for
spinners 2

Introduction   **4**

Choosing the fiber 6 / Sheep breeds and grades 7 / How
much fiber should I buy? 8 / Making the yarn 9 / Dye
solutions 19 / Applying the dyes 19

Equipment . . . and connections   **21**

Designing with handspun yarns   **24**

Solid-color yarns 24 / Variegated yarns 25 / Novelty
yarns 25 / Special fibers 25

Getting ready to knit   **28**

Making the right size 28 / Determining yarn quantities 29 /
Knitting terms 30 / Knitting techniques 31

THE PATTERNS: 24 Outstanding Sweaters   **33**

1 Fair Isle Pullover 35
2 Novelty Yarn Pullover 37
3 Linen Jacket 43
4 Tweed Pullover 46
5 Island Fleece Pullover 51
6 Silk and Angora Pullover 56
7 Angora Eyelet Pullover 60
8 Bohus Cardigan 64
9 Dressy Pullover in Naturals 69
10 Camel and Silk Vest 75
11 Fair Isle Vest 77
12 & 13 Shetland Vest and Cardigan 81
14 Cotswold Pullover 87
15 Silk and Wool Pullover 90

16 Variegated Vest 95
17 Merino Cardigan 99
18 Silk and Linen Pullover 103
19 Welsh Mountain Pullover 105
20 Mohair Cardigan 111
21 Pictorial Pullover 115
22 Finn Double Vest 119
23 Diagonal Vest 124
24 Icelandic Pullover 129

Conclusion 132

Acknowledgments 133 / Fiber, dye, and equipment sources
134 / Bibliography 137

Index 139

Preface

When two designers get together and start exchanging ideas, there are soon so many ideas that it's logical to want to share them. That's how this book came about. It is a mere beginning, a guide to help you forge ahead with your spinning and knitting creations. For non-spinning knitters, it's an introduction to the joys of handspun yarn.

Many of the styles are classics which will remain favorites for years. Some are more contemporary, for a change of pace—although we think these, too, will stand the test of time. The fibers and spinning techniques are varied, and can often be interchanged. We offer a wide range of adult sizes, and lots of other useful information for the knitter and spinner.

It would be a thrill for us to see a sweater that you have made from the ideas in this book. But it would be a bigger thrill to see a sweater that you have designed through understanding the approach that we offer. Make this book your own!

A special note for non-spinners

All the styles designed for this book have been made with handspun yarn. They can be made in commercial yarns, or you may want to discover the pleasures of handspun. Here are some hints which will help you make successful substitutions.

When selecting a commercially spun yarn, you will increase your chances of obtaining a fabric similar to ours if you match the fiber content as closely as possible. In any case, you must be able to match the gauge indicated on each individual pattern. Although handspun yarns don't come in standard sizes, we have given each of our yarns a size designation which relates to commercial sizes. We have used the terms *sport, light worsted, worsted, light bulky,* and *bulky.* If you are an experienced knitter, you will be able to proceed from there; and if you need guidance, a knowledgeable staff person at a yarn shop should be able to help you find equivalents.

If you are attracted to a style because of the special dyeing or spinning process used, you may find it more challenging to locate a substitute yarn. Most yarn companies manufacture a variety of novelty yarns, but they tend to be available only seasonally and for brief

1

periods. Consequently, we can't recommend specific types. Again, you may need to rely on the people at your local yarn shop. Even if they don't stock an appropriate yarn, they have catalogs and sample books and are familiar with their contents. They should be able to help you discover whether a suitable substitute exists.

Of course, we have to admit that the best way to obtain the exact yarn required is to find an experienced spinner who can make it for you. Although this may be more costly than simply buying balls of commercial yarn, the finished garment will be worth far more than it would have been, and it will be truly one-of-a-kind!

You may find that working with handspun yarns is so rewarding that you want to guarantee your own supply by learning to spin. If you reach this point, you will find additional benefits, since the community of spinners is a special group of people. Many local yarn shops and craft centers offer spinning classes, or know of local spinners who might be able to teach you. Depending on your abilities and your ambition, you could spin yarn for a sweater after your first set of spinning classes. However, people spin because they *like* to spin, and not just to acquire yarn. It is pleasant work, but it does take time!

An introductory note for spinners

We've chosen to design sweaters which aren't too difficult, either in spinning or knitting, and to give instructions which will allow you to streamline the process or to customize it further, as you choose. Although we emphasize wool, we also have ramie, linen, silk, camel, and a variety of other fibers. We do not include cotton, but if you are proficient at spinning that fiber the designs intended for the other less resilient fibers will be appropriate. We give a lot of suggestions for substituting fibers, preparation methods, and colors. Don't forget to play.

To help you plan your approach, we kept some records. Each sweater in this book involved at least twenty hours of preparation, spinning, and dyeing for Rachael, who is an experienced spinner (the most time-consuming required fifty hours). Nibbling steadily at your project, at the rate of an hour or two a day, will bring you to completion in a reasonable period of time. As a by-product, this steady progress will give you increased confidence . . . and the habit of spinning regularly.

You'll find that as your skills increase, so will the thrill of having these special garments in your wardrobe.

Introduction

This book is about spinning the yarn you want, dyeing it the perfect color, and knitting a wonderful sweater which will stay in your wardrobe for years and perhaps be handed along to the next generation. The sweaters vary in complexity. We have kept the required skill levels within reach of the beginning-to-intermediate spinner and knitter; we hope our approach to designing will be useful to the more experienced as well. Some of the designs begin with raw fibers, some with processed. Some require dyeing, some don't. Some contain pattern stitches, some are based on stockinette. Each will serve you well.

You may or may not perform all the steps of making these garments yourself—you don't have to. The sweaters may inspire you to combine your talents with those of a friend or to discover a new acquaintance whose skills complement yours. You can buy prepared or dyed fibers to spin from, or locate a commercial yarn which approximates our original. You can get involved in the process to any extent you want.

If there's one thing we'd like you to gain from this book, it's a sense of joy and accomplishment, whether you're a spinner, a knitter, or both. Yarn is such an infinitely variable thing, and knitting contains so many more possibilities than anyone could explore in a single lifetime, that the methods and designs we offer only hint at the possibilities. The most important parts of this book may be our descriptions of how we arrived at our decisions, and of the alternatives we didn't have time to explore.

Rachael is a spinner who also knits; Hélène, a knitter who is learning to spin. While we understand each other's strengths, the collaboration which produced this book did two things. It allowed us to capitalize on our individual proficiencies and to imagine garments and then *make* them—no hunting for the right weight of yarn, in the correct fiber, and an inspiring color. It also permitted us to explore our collaboration—for you, the parallel could be your collaboration with another person, or between the spinner and the knitter within you. We got to examine first-hand how yarn design influences sweater design, and vice versa. Our individual notes on the sweaters tell you what we discovered.

Rachael

Hélène

Having this much control produced a new liveliness in our designs and encouraged us to explore our versatility. Producing this many sweaters in a short time-span (just about a year) engaged us in a healthy stretching process. Whether you make one vest or a dozen different projects, we think you will discover the same benefits.

Yarn: the essential ingredient

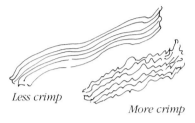

Less crimp   *More crimp*

Whether you have done some spinning or are a knitter who wants to understand yarn better, this section will give you an overview of the decisions and processes which are required to make a good yarn. The texts we list in the bibliography go into much greater depth on the "how-tos" of spinning. Our main goal here is to instill in non-spinners an appreciation for quality yarn, and to cue spinners in to our own preferences for spinning techniques.

Choosing the fiber

You can't make a soft, dressy sweater out of a stiff fiber like Karakul wool, any more than you can produce a sturdy ski pullover from angora. When you first begin to think about designing a garment, you need to consider the basic characteristics of the fiber you will work with. These are its *size*, its *crimp*, its *length*, and its *luster*. Handspinners have access to a much wider range of fibers than can be efficiently processed commercially; one of the major advantages to making your own yarn (or buying handspun) is that you can have better control over the characteristics of your yarn. You can design the yarn to complement your sweater design, and vice versa.

Size refers to whether the fiber is fine or coarse. All fibers look fine compared to a pencil, but compared to each other there are differences equally profound. Some fibers are fine (and consequently soft) enough for use in baby wear, while others are coarse (and durable) enough to be used in rugs. And of course all the territory between these extremes is covered as well.

Crimp is the waviness in a fiber's profile. Fibers have more or less crimp, and as a result are more or less elastic. For example, a very crimpy Merino wool is very elastic, while a Karakul, with little or no crimp, makes a stiff, inelastic yarn. As a general rule, fine fibers have more crimp than coarse ones.

Its *length* determines, to some extent, how easy a fiber is to spin. The beginning spinner may have trouble with either very short or very long fibers. A good length range to start out with is between 3 and 5 inches. Longer fibers tend to be the coarser types, while shorter fibers are often finer. Sheep breeders who are aware of handspinners'

6

needs are working to produce fine, soft fleeces with long fibers.

Luster, or the shininess of a fiber, may become important for evening wear (although you'll want to watch the associated coarseness, and be sure your garment is also comfortable to wear) or when you'd like the light-reflective quality of the fiber itself to make your dyed colors appear richer. Luster shows up most obviously in fibers with less crimp. For example, Merino, a fine, crimpy fiber, is not noted for its luster. Romney, with less crimp, has higher luster.

The four fiber characteristics go hand-in-hand, from:

fine to coarse
very crimpy to less crimpy
short to long
matte to lustrous.

These progressions are easiest to see in wool.

Sheep breeds and grades

We can only give a general guide to sheep breeds, because breeders are creating new and exciting crossbreeds every year. Spinners learn through experience to judge individual fleeces by feel. This awareness extends to an ability to evaluate the qualities of commercial yarns, as well.

Wools from the following breeds are used in this book. Breeds are listed from finest-wooled to coarsest-wooled:

Merino
Shetland
Finn
Corriedale
Romney/Perendale
Maine Island fleeces
Mixed-breed carded wool
Welsh Mountain
Cotswold
Icelandic

We selected a wide range of different types of wools; the Merino is very fine, while the wools from Welsh Mountain through Icelandic are noticeably coarse. The intermediate types give a good idea of the range of wools to be discovered in between. However, like most spinners, we didn't limit ourselves to wool. Wool is usually easiest to spin, although you'll find that by selecting carefully you can branch out into other fibers early in your spinning experience. Cotton is notoriously challenging, so we haven't included it here.

Silk is the finest natural fiber available, with angora and camel down close behind. Silk, because of the length of its fibers, can be reasonably easy to spin. Both angora and camel down have short fibers, but once you make the acquaintance of these materials in handspun form you'll be motivated to try them.

As plant-derived fibers, linen and ramie are about mid-range in coarseness. Linen fibers can be extremely long; even in commercially processed form, linen usually has longer fibers than ramie, and is therefore somewhat easier to spin. Ramie makes a beautiful yarn that feels something like a cross between cotton and linen.

Mohair, which is the hair of Angora goats, can vary widely in size. It can be very coarse or extremely fine, depending on the breeding, feeding, and age of the animal from which it was shorn. "Kid" mohair, from young goats, is the finest.

How much fiber should I buy?

Some of the sweaters in this book have been made with commercially cleaned and processed fibers. For others, we began with raw wool. The individual knitting instructions for each garment indicate the finished weight of each type of yarn which you will need for the size of sweater you want to make. With clean, processed fibers, the amount to buy will be slightly more than the completed weight of yarn because there will be very little waste. For raw fibers, calculating quantities is a matter of educated guesswork.

Generally a fleece's raw weight in proportion to the finished (washed and/or scoured) weight, will vary considerably, depending on the breed of sheep, the age and health of the particular animal, the weather, the shearer's skill, and the quantities of dirt, manure, waxes, and oils involved. This suggests that at best it is difficult to specify or guess precise fleece quantities for a project. Our suggestion would be to add one third to one half extra weight to finished project requirements. For example, if a project requires 24 ounces add 8 to 12 ounces in raw weight and buy 32-36 ounces of raw fleece. If your fiber is not readily repeatable, as in the case of individual Shetland fleeces, order more rather than less for extra weight. It is better to have leftovers for mittens or sweater accents than not to be able to finish a sleeve top.

To give you an idea of our experience, we were able to buy precisely the weight required when we used scoured wool top, since there was no waste. We found that the finished yarn made of Icelandic fleece weighed half of its raw fleece amount (for this particular fleece, the rough guidelines and general rule above are too conservative). You'll notice in some of our notes that we ran out of fiber and had to acquire more. In the case of sweater 3 (Linen Jacket) we were working with commercially dyed fiber and had to mix dyelots. There are, as we explain, ways to do this so no one will ever know.

Making the yarn

It's a good idea to sample before you go to the trouble of making *all* the yarn for a garment. Make up singles, ply them if you think plying is suitable, and work a sample in your finished technique or stitch. Spin and knit a swatch! Your yarn may work better as a single strand, a two-ply, a three-ply, or you may decide it needs an extra "zip" of color. Use your swatches to check out both spinning techniques and design ideas. Make your "second-best" efforts early and in small quantities. Then go first class for your garment.

In outlining Rachael's methods of making yarn, we'll start at the beginning, as if we were choosing and working with a raw fleece. If you'll be working with processed fibers for your first project, skim the first steps and start paying serious attention where it says "Pulling," below.

Rachael is the kind of person who does each step completely as she comes to it. Then she goes on to the next step. Through years of experience, she has developed a technique for handling raw fleece which is careful and efficient without being overly time-consuming.

Spinning is not, however, a rush activity. Time spent in preparation eliminates aggravation at spinning time. To be able to make a smooth yarn, you need a smooth, clean fiber supply. In addition, monitor the quality of your yarn and, while spinning to relax is a good idea, don't spin when you're overtired. By the end of a four-hour spinning session your concentration will flag and it is time for a substantial break.

Picking a fleece: This does not mean choosing it; you have already done that. It *does* mean opening up the fiber clumps to allow bits of straw and seed and dirt to fall out. A thorough picking prepares the fiber for more successful washing or scouring. Work systematically through the wool making sure the debris falls out of the way, and not into your wool supply.

Washing: Washing removes accumulated dirt from the fibers, while scouring removes both dirt and the wool's protective coating (waxes and lanolin). If you remove only the dirt, the naturally occurring waxes and lanolin remain on the wool so you can make a semi-water-resistant garment. Some commercial yarns sold for use in fishermen's sweaters retain the waxes and lanolin. However, it's good to remember that too much lanolin left in a garment can cause it to stiffen in the cold outdoors and become uncomfortable.

Washing can be done in several different ways. Generally, washing wool involves the use of cool-to-warm water and a mild soap or mild detergent, along with lots of rinsing.

When you spin wool that contains lanolin, you may find it easier to spin on a warm day or near a heat source which will keep the fibers flexible. You may want to spin a washed fleece soon after you clean it; in storage, the lanolin can oxidize and make the fleece gummy and hard to spin. If you have a fleece you know you will need to store, or you have stored one and it has gotten tacky, the solution is to scour the wool.

Scouring: This more rigorous cleaning removes dirt, vegetation, waxes, and lanolin. It requires hot water and a mild but concentrated

Always treat wet wool gently. Sometimes stubborn clumps can be eased apart while the wool is being washed.

Wet, clean fleece.

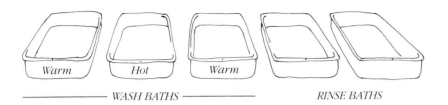

Warm   Hot   Warm

———— WASH BATHS ————   RINSE BATHS

Teasing wool opens the clumps of fiber.

Carding helps you produce a controlled yarn which contains lumps only if you want them.

detergent. We use Synthrapol[SP], a wetting and pre-scouring agent (see list of sources).

Prepare a series of five baths:

1. *Warm water with a little detergent.* In this bath, you get the dirt out.

2. *Hot water with a lot of detergent.* This is the critical bath in which the waxes are removed.

3. *Warm water with a little detergent.*

4 & 5. *Clear warm water* (rinse baths).

Gently lay and lift handfuls of picked wool through these baths, in order, then lay the wool out to dry.[1] You can speed the drying process if you contain the wool in net bags or old pillowcases and run it through the *spin only* cycle of a washing machine before spreading it on towels to finish drying.

Teasing: This step looks a lot like picking except that fibers are separated from each other, where in picking the clumps of fiber were simply opened. At this stage you will pull handfuls of fiber completely apart. Thorough teasing results in easier carding.

Carding: Fibers need to be opened out fully or aligned, so you can produce a controlled yarn. Snarled fibers produce lumpy yarn. It's important to prepare fleece well even if you want to make a textured yarn, since the texture should be controlled by the spinner, not the wool.

There are two reasonable ways to card wool for handspinning: with hand cards or a drum carder. (Wool combs provide an alternative which we don't cover, since the equipment is expensive, less readily available, and requires a different type of skill to use. We do use commercially combed top in some designs.) The small bunch of fiber produced by hand cards is called a *rolag*, while a drum carder processes a larger amount of fiber into a *batt*.

The two basic arrangements we use for spinning in this book are called *woolen* and *semi-worsted*. For semi-worsted yarns, the fibers

[1]For a more detailed description of scouring, see Allen Fannin's *Handspinning: Art and Technique.*

Rolag rolled for woolen spinning.

Batt from drum carder.

Batt rolled for woolen spinning.

Rolag rolled for semi-worsted spinning.

Batt rolled for semi-worsted spinning.

are kept as close to parallel as possible; the rolag is removed from the card by rolling it parallel to its side edge, or the batt is rolled up parallel to its long edge. For woolen yarns, the fibers run in all directions; the rolag is formed by rolling from the toe to the heel of the card, and the batt is rolled from its short edge.

Blending: Some special effects can be produced only by blending fibers of different colors, lengths, or types. We've used all three combinations in this book. Blending is easiest to do on a drum carder.

If you intend, for example, to blend two types of fiber, start by carding the entire supply of one of the kinds. Then lay these batts on a flat surface. Distribute the second type of fiber on top of the spread-out batts, then card each batt again to produce the mix. You may need to card these blended groups several times; one carding will leave some color or texture variation in the fiber, while multiple cardings will produce a more thoroughly blended, and therefore homogeneous, yarn.

Pulling: Not all spinners pull their carded fibers or rovings before spinning, but this simple task can save a lot of time and make spinning much more pleasurable. Pulling just means drawing out the fiber to a size closer to that of the singles you want to make. If you intend to make a fine yarn, you will pull the fiber to a finer dimension than if you want to make a heavy yarn.

Work down the length of the fiber package with your hands a little distance apart; the idea is to pull evenly and not to make thick and thin spots. If you let the pulled fiber drop into a basket, it will be contained and handy. A basket of pulled fiber all ready to spin is a pleasant sight; you will be amazed at how quickly it will become yarn. When you are ready to spin, turn the yarn over in the basket and begin to spin at the end where you started pulling; this will produce a smoother yarn.

Spinning draws: Spinning is a matter of sliding fibers past each other until you get the desired thickness of fibers for your yarn, and then allowing those fibers to twist together so they stay put. Your

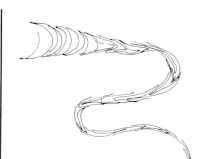
Fibers prepared for woolen spinning run in all directions.

Fibers prepared for semi-worsted spinning are kept as close to parallel as possible.

Pulling saves time and makes the spinning go smoothly.

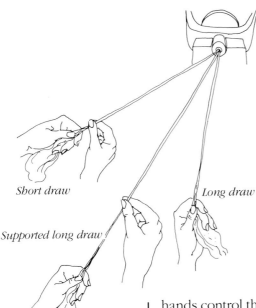

Short draw

Long draw

Supported long draw

hands control the sliding of the fibers; your wheel does the twisting, although you keep it under constant control. A *draw* is a method of accomplishing this sliding and twisting, and spinning books describe different methods. In addition, different spinners sometimes have different names for the same technique. The following are the terms used in this book and what is meant by them.

Short draw. This is the inching along that beginning spinners resort to when they're afraid the yarn will get away from them. It's also a legitimate draw under some circumstances. The fiber is drawn out between the two hands; the front hand pinches the yarn and holds back the twist from the wheel while the back hand slides along and gets the fiber ready to be twisted. When the front hand releases its grip, the twist moves back and makes yarn.

Sliding short draw. This is a modification of the short draw, for use with short, slippery fibers. The same motions occur, but the yarn is allowed to slip more readily through the forward hand. Sliding draws, long and short, are also good for fibers you aren't accustomed to.

Supported long draw. This is the technique we use for most fibers. The back hand draws out while the front hand pinches off the twist, as in the short draw, although the hands are held farther apart. In addition, a small amount of twist is allowed to pass into the fiber between the hands after it is initially drawn out—just enough to give that area a little strength, but not so much that the fibers cannot still be drawn out farther. Then the fibers are drawn to their finished length and the full amount of twist is allowed to enter the yarn.

Sliding long draw. This goes one slight movement beyond the supported long draw, in that the forward hand is constantly sliding as needed for yarn production.

Long draw. Here the front hand is eliminated; the technique is, of course, ideal for use on the great wheel, where one hand is occupied in turning the wheel itself. Using one hand only (usually the left), draw out the fiber at a rate compatible with the twist being provided by the wheel. You will draft with the newly twisted yarn itself providing the resistance. If you plan to use this technique, your fiber must be well-prepared so it will draw out smoothly with little intervention on your part.

Singles and plying: First, you spin *singles*; plying is putting two or more singles together to make a fatter, stronger, or fancier yarn. Generally, singles are spun with Z twist, by turning the wheel clockwise, and yarns are plied with S twist, by turning the wheel counterclockwise. There are many exceptions to this, but our focus is on simple and interesting handspun yarns and this basic principle will serve you well.

A good knitting yarn is often a *balanced* yarn, in which the Z twist of the singles and the S twist of the plying action are present in amounts which balance each other. This is easier to do than it sounds. Once you understand the concept, you'll get the feeling for this type of yarn in your fingers and you can work from trained intuition, with an occasional mathematical check.

First, you need to know how many twists are put into your yarn for every turn of your driving wheel. This number is frequently called the *wheel ratio.* You can figure it out by measuring the distances around (1) your driving wheel and (2) the groove at the end of your bobbin or flyer (sometimes—but not usually—both), and comparing the results. For example, if a driving wheel measures 60" and the end of the bobbin measures 6", you have a 10-to-1 ratio. For every complete turn of the big wheel, the yarn will receive 10 twists.

What that means for the yarn being made depends on how many inches those 10 twists get packed into. Ten twists in 1" make a firmer yarn than 10 twists in 4" (assuming the same weight of yarn). If you treadle five times for a length of 8", you will have 50 twists for the 8", or a little over 6 twists per inch (abbreviated *t.p.i.*). You simply count the times you treadle, estimate the number of inches of yarn formed, and you can determine how many t.p.i. you're putting into your singles.

s-twist   *z-twist*

How do you tell if your wheel is bobbin-lead or flyer-lead? Look to see whether the drive band turns the flyer or the bobbin.

If you have a *double* drive which turns *both* flyer and bobbin, take measurements on the driving wheel and flyer grooves.

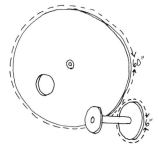

On a bobbin-lead wheel, compare the measurement of the driving wheel to the measurement of the bobbin groove. If both ends of the bobbin are grooved, you have a choice of two ratios.

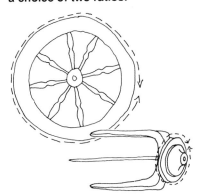

On a flyer-lead wheel, compare the measurement of the driving wheel to the measurement of the flyer groove.

When it's time to ply, you can achieve a balanced yarn by plying two singles with $1/2$ to $2/3$ the number of t.p.i. that were used in the singles. If there were a little over 6 t.p.i. in the singles, make a balanced two-ply yarn by using between 3 and 4 t.p.i.

How much twist *should* you put into your singles? That depends on how hard or soft a yarn you want, which in turn depends on the fiber you're using and what you're making. In general, you want a soft twist for a luxury or special-event garment, and hard twist for children's wear and rugged outdoor garments. Sampling and experience are the best guides.

For example, the same fleece could be spun several ways, as follows:

For socks that will last indefinitely, spin singles at between 12-18 t.p.i., ply at 6-9 t.p.i. Be careful that the yarn in this case doesn't become too "boardy" and thus uncomfortable to wear.

For medium-weight sweaters, spin singles at 6-8 t.p.i, ply at 3-4 t.p.i. Slight variations here will make a slightly softer or firmer sweater; use a little less twist to soften the yarn, and a little more to make it harder. The feel of your knitted fabric will also be affected by the needle size you select and the resulting gauge, so remember to sample before you start the final project.

For lofty yarns or baby-soft garments, spin singles at 3-4 t.p.i., ply at 2 t.p.i. Be aware that softly-spun yarns, though comfortable, do not necessarily stand up well to heavy use. The risks are pilling and thinning of vulnerable areas, like elbows.

Our Icelandic sweater (number 24) contains the softest yarn in this collection; the hardest yarn appears in the Fair Isle sweater (number 1).

Consistency of your yarn is very important. Wrap samples of spun yarn, both singles and plied, around a stiff support (cardboard or a book) and keep it near your spinning wheel for constant reference and comparison. By itself, however, this guide will not insure that you make a consistent yarn. You need to remember to use it.

Finishing and measuring the yarn: All yarn to be used for knitting should be finished with a final washing before you cast on. By

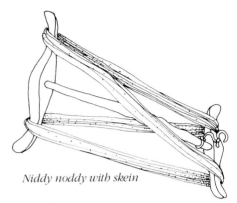

Niddy noddy with skein

lightly cleaning it in warm-to-hot water with detergent, and then thoroughly rinsing, you set the twist and prepare the yarn to be made up into a garment that can be washed without shrinking.

After it is spun, you will wind it into skeins on a niddy noddy or other device which might be a skein winder, the end of a table, a couple of chairs, or whatever else imagination provides. Although a niddy noddy might measure 2 yards around, the finished skeins relax and do not measure a full 2 yards. When the yarn is washed, it contracts a little more. The original 72" (2-yard) skein may measure 66" or less, depending on the fiber.

After your finished skein is dry, measure it and figure how much yardage you have produced. A simple formula:

skein size × number of turns in the skein = inches of yarn,
÷ 36 = number of yards in the skein

Spinning to gauge: The patterns in this book suggest a yarn that is spun at a certain number of yards per pound. We offer a lot of suggestions to help you spin a comparable yarn. Consider the following:

What weight is the yarn?
How many plies are there?
Is it a lofty yarn?
How many twists per inch are in the singles?

Look at the photographs of the yarns, which are as close to actual size as we can make them. Then measure out one ounce of fiber, spin it as the guidelines indicate, skein it, wash it, allow it to dry, and measure the yardage. Multiplied by 16, this one-ounce measurement will give you yards per pound. Compare your yarn to the picture. Do you need to spin lighter or heavier singles? Do you need a little more or less twist? Adjust your spinning accordingly.

You can make our yarns with commercially dyed fiber, or you can take control and produce fantastic colors yourself. There are many types of dyes on the market. We have used simple dyes that are relatively easy to find, but which give good results. "Good" means you can control the color, and it will be reasonably fast to light and washing. We have given enough information so that you will be able to complete the project at hand. For more complete general dye information, try Linda Knutson's *Synthetic Dyes for Natural Fibers*. Our dye methods are among the simplest available; we have not used some optional chemicals which promote even dyeing, both to keep the dyeing process simple and because we don't believe perfectly even dyelots are always necessary.

We have chosen to work with chemical rather than "natural" dyes. With children in the house, it is necessary to exercise extreme caution with the harsh, toxic chemicals used as mordants in natural dyeing. Small amounts of chemical dyes are less dangerous, which is not to say that chemical dyeing is totally safe. *It is not!* However, with care it can be compatible with family life. Gloves, special dyepots and tools, good ventilation, and careful storage of dye solutions are essential.

The dyestuff you select must suit both the fiber you will dye and the effect you want to produce.

Cushing's dye is an all-purpose type, and can be successfully used on a broad range of fibers. It is readily available in craft and spinning shops. Instructions are on the package. For single projects, it is inexpensive, and it comes in a broad range of mixed colors. It is not as washfast or as lightfast as the other dyes we use in this book.

We used two different brands of acid dyes, which require the use of vinegar or acetic acid to help the dye adhere to the fiber. Acid dyes are appropriate for wool and other animal fibers, including silk.

Craftsman's dye is an acid dye in powder form, available in small amounts from mail-order sources. Either vinegar or acetic acid can be used with Craftsman's dyes, which we obtained from The Ruggery. There are eleven basic colors, and The Ruggery publishes a brochure telling how to mix other colors and how to use the dyes on materials for rugs. The same procedure works on raw wool fiber or yarn.

PRO washfast acid dyes, from PRO Chemical and Dye, are easy to use with acetic acid as an assistant, and come in a good range of colors for mixing. You can get a beginner's dye sample kit. The manufacturer supplies instructions in its catalog and instruction sheets for each of its dyes.

Fiber-reactive dyes are designed for use on cotton and other plant fibers, and also work on silk. Their colors become fast without the use of hot water; soaking in warm water is adequate. The Procion H dyes we used, also from PRO Chemical and Dye, can be combined with a print paste that helps you place dye pigment exactly where you want it, which comes in handy when you paint yarns. This paste contains both the soda needed to set the dye and a thickener to make it a more controllable consistency. For pot dyeing, soda must be added to the dyebath to make the color chemically bond to the fiber. Buy your soda from the dye supplier rather than from the grocery store, since the grocery store variety has bleaches or other chemicals added.

Telana dyes (formerly called Lanaset) give strong, even color on silks and wools. The dyeing process is longer than for our other dyes, involving more careful timing and additional chemicals, but for a special project over which you want complete control, the effort pays off. The supplier, Cerulean Blue, offers excellent instructions in its catalog and on individual instruction sheets.

Generally, if you want to do a small project or if you dye infrequently, Cushing's and Craftsman's dyes are most convenient. Although most dye companies offer small packages, the occasional dyer uses what is at hand—whether the supply comes from a friend's well-stocked dye closet, from the dime store (Rit®), or a kitchen cupboard (Kool-Aid® or Jello®).

A more serious dyer should choose one basic dye and become familiar with its variables. Certain colors will "take" at specific temperatures. You can develop a sense for accurate color mixing with a dye you know well. Of course, careful notes are invaluable as you experiment with dyestuffs.

Rubber gloves keep your hands free of dye; the stock solution is stored in a well-labeled jar. Set dye jars down on foam meat-trays to make sure the dyes go only where you want them.

Dye solutions

Generally for acid dyes, use one tablespoon in one pint of boiling water for a 1% solution. This jar of stock solution can then be measured in whichever way seems appropriate: medicine droppers and graduates that measure milliliters can be used, or some days a teaspoon or tablespoon seems more convenient. Of course, be sure to keep notes about the dyes combined and the quantities used. However, a good general approach is to trust your eye.

When working with other dye systems, like Lanaset, weigh out prescribed amounts for the stock solutions, as suggested in the supplier's instructions, and proceed as they recommend. Instructions are given with each sweater in this book, but you may wish to know more if dyeing really captures your interest.

Applying the dyes

Our notes on the sweaters give you specific information on how dyes were applied. Only a few general notes are necessary here. You can dye either fiber (before spinning) or yarn. You'll get different effects depending on when you add the color.

Before you begin to use any dyes, *read the instructions*, paying special attention to safety notes. *Keep pots and utensils used for dyeing separate from your kitchen equipment, and do not use them for food. Always wear rubber gloves to handle dye and, if possible, use a face mask when handling dye powders.*

When you dye unspun fiber, observing some simple precautions will keep the fiber from being overly agitated and turning into felt. When using roving or top, wind the fiber into a skein and tie it together loosely in at least four places. When you're dyeing fleece, you can place the open locks directly in the dyepot and handle them gently through the stirring and rinsing processes. This careful handling will not necessarily result in a perfectly even dye job, although you can use this to your advantage. Blend the fiber when you card or spin; it will appear to have been evenly dyed, but the color will have some extra liveliness.

When you choose to dye yarn, make skeins of equal sizes and tie them loosely in several places. For even dyeing, small skeins work best.

Always handle fibers gently when you stir and rinse them, and don't allow abrupt changes of water temperature—it's better to risk having a slightly uneven dye job than to find you've made felt. Slight variations in color in unspun fiber can be blended in when you card or spin, and will give your yarn more life and color depth.

Dyeing fiber unevenly on purpose will give you a mix of values or colors. Uneven dyeing comes from breaking the "rules." You tie your skeins tightly, put your fiber in a pot with barely enough water to cover it, pour the dye directly onto the fiber, and do not stir at all. And of course, record what you did.

Once your fiber's the right color, you're almost finished. Complete and careful rinsing is important to any dye job, since it helps remove any residual dye. Whenever you dye, make careful notes of what you did on full-sized paper; scraps get lost!

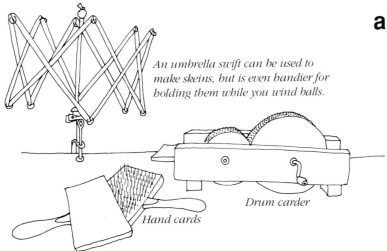

An umbrella swift can be used to make skeins, but is even handier for holding them while you wind balls.

Drum carder

Hand cards

Spinning and dyeing do require special equipment. As a beginner, you may be able to share with a friend, but as your interests grow you will want your own tools.

Carding. For hand cards, start with basic, medium-grade wool cards. As you handle finer fibers, you will want to add fine-grade (also called "cotton") cards. A drum carder costs significantly more; it processes your fiber more quickly, but does not eliminate the need for hand cards for special blending and small projects. Drum carders can be supplied with varying grades of card clothing (fine, medium, or coarse). Some come with interchangeable drums so you can select the correct carding level for a particular fiber. Before you decide which equipment to buy, evaluate the features of several companies' products (this will be a refrain throughout the equipment section).

A wheel. By far the most important piece of equipment, it should be versatile enough to allow you to spin many types of fibers and sizes of yarn. There are many wheels available. It is worth locating spinners' guilds and conferences in order to try different kinds. A Canadian or Quebec wheel or a flax wheel is great for spinning a fine yarn, but check the size of the orifice (the hole through which yarns travel on their way to the bobbin). It may be too small for bulky singles or even medium-weight plied yarns. A small number of wheels have a hook in place of the orifice, which expands the range of sizes that can be spun.

Indian spinners, on the other hand, permit the spinning of super-bulky yarns, but do not lend themselves to the production of fine yarns.

A great wheel is just that, a great wheel! This is the kind with a very large driving wheel and a spindle, instead of a flyer assembly. It offers many spinning possibilities. However, you must be able to use the long draw method of spinning and be willing to fully prepare your spinning fiber—and, in most cases, be able to spin standing up. The more typical flyer wheel, with a foot treadle to provide the power, is probably your best bet for a "first" wheel.

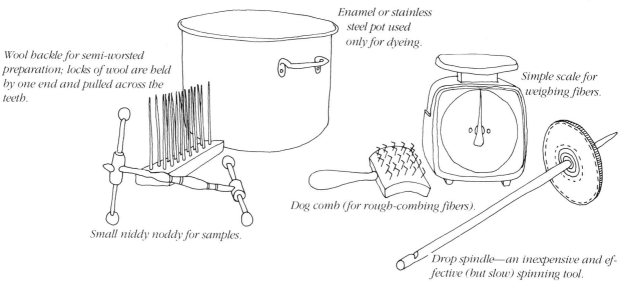

Wool hackle for semi-worsted preparation; locks of wool are held by one end and pulled across the teeth.

Enamel or stainless steel pot used only for dyeing.

Simple scale for weighing fibers.

Dog comb (for rough-combing fibers).

Small niddy noddy for samples.

Drop spindle—an inexpensive and effective (but slow) spinning tool.

The yarns for this book were spun on a Louët. It is a versatile wheel on which it is possible to produce yarns from very fine to quite bulky, simply by repositioning the bobbin. The ball-bearing mechanism allows long-term use without leg fatigue. The feel and efficiency of a wheel are very important; look for similar qualities in wheels you are considering. The biggest question is, *Are you comfortable while spinning?* This can take some time to discover, so try to arrange for trials which allow you that leisure.

For most of us, price enters into decision-making. Fortunately, the most expensive wheel is not necessarily the best. However, remember that quality equipment will have a quality price tag. This shouldn't scare you, but instead may force you to be clear about what you want and may require that you wait a few more months to save up for the right wheel.

Do your homework and try many different wheels. Borrow or rent several types if you can.

Evaluate your own interests. Do you like to work with fine yarns, mediums, or bulkies?

Do be careful when buying a secondhand wheel. It is being sold for a reason; find out what that reason is. The wheel may not work at all, it may work unpleasantly, or, if you are lucky, the seller has simply decided to upgrade or move in another direction. There *are* spinning wheels which are good only for use as planters.

Other equipment. A niddy noddy or skein winder is handy for getting your yarn from the bobbin into a skein, so you may wash and/or dye it. There are lots of different styles; although these are much less expensive tools than spinning wheels, try several varieties if you can. Some work more smoothly, or are more aesthetically pleasing.

A scale becomes important when you want to repeat dye formulas or yarn weights. Again, research the different styles. Accuracy is important, so look for this quality and be prepared to pay for it. The degree of accuracy you require will, however, depend upon the level of precision you consider desirable.

You will need one or two special pots to be used for dyeing only. Garage or tag sales can sometimes turn up bargains. You will also

Special tools and containers for dyestuffs only.

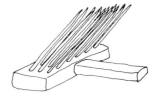

Wool comb (used in pairs).

need to have a separate supply of stirring sticks, measuring cups, and spoons. Mark all this equipment clearly and store it out of the kitchen so your family does not borrow it for a cooking project.

These are the basics; there are many other pieces of equipment you may need as your interests become clear and your skills develop. Flickers, wool combs, the many kinds of drop and supported spindles, an antique flax wheel, an Indian spinner, a great wheel or a charkha . . . the possibilities are nearly endless. Some people find a mechanical ball winder to be indispensable.

Books and magazines are invaluable tools. Be willing to research a new technique or fiber and then try it yourself. By checking what other people have written, you can see how they have used the fiber, compare it to your current practice, then add, expand, change, and make that fiber your own. National periodicals, like those listed in the appendix, contain advertisements for dyes, fibers, equipment, and books. They also sometimes run evaluation columns. The brochures and samples offered by advertisers will expand your awareness of what's available and how it might help you meet your goals.

Your local spinning supplier or craft shop can also offer information. One or more staff members may be particularly knowledgeable.

Connections. One of the best things about spinning is the people. They can help you in your quest for equipment . . . and information. Look for a local spinning group (a list of groups and guilds is published annually in *Spin·Off,* with updates every issue), or start one with an ad in your newspaper. Something as simple as "People interested in spinning and forming an informal spinning group, please call 555-5678" may leave you pleasantly surprised at finding other spinners in your area.

Designing with handspun yarns

When you're designing a sweater, the yarn can demand attention or the sweater's construction can be dominant. Our sweater concepts are based on a balance between fine yarn construction and sweater design. We could have chosen to produce more intricate novelty yarns, and to design very simple sweater constructions which would be compatible with them. The yarns are interesting but not extremely demanding to make. The sweaters are classic, with distinctive touches.

Sometimes we designed the yarn first; in other instances, we had a sweater idea and produced the yarn we felt would most effectively complement it. When working with yarns, whether smooth and solidly colored or thick-and-thin and variegated, there's always the challenge of selecting just the right style and knitting stitch(es) to result in a completely satisfying sweater. Our notes on the individual sweaters will tell you where our ideas came from and how we developed them.

Getting the combinations right involves spending a little time knitting samples until the best decisions become clear. Some of our general guidelines may help you with your designing.

Solid-color yarns

Smooth two-ply: This is the most commonly spun type of yarn. It is an all-purpose structure which works well with textured knitting stitches and, when made in several colors, for charted designs (see sweater 1, Fair Isle Pullover). Spun in sport or worsted weight, a smooth two-ply works well in lace patterns. This type of yarn can be particularly attractive when slight color variations are achieved through dyeing (see the notes for sweaters 11 and 12, the Shetland Sweater Set).

Smooth three-ply: This is a rounded yarn which can be used in place of a smooth two-ply, but it is particularly well suited to cable work and high relief stitches (see sweater 5, Island Fleece Pullover). It gives the stitches strong definition.

Smooth singles: This type can be used much as the smooth two-ply, as a good all-around yarn. Be careful, though, not to overtwist it when you spin, since an overtwisted singles can cause the knitted fabric to *bias*, or become distorted (a rectangle will end up leaning like the Tower of Pisa, and no amount of blocking will bring it upright).

Variegated yarns

Variegated yarns can be smooth-textured or novelty-type yarns. If the texture is smooth and the color is the design emphasis, you may find that your fabric develops unintentional stripes. If you don't like this effect, you should know that it is most noticeable in stockinette, and the selection of an all-over textured stitch may ease the problem (see sweater 15, Variegated Vest).

Additional techniques, such as working the garment from side to side or on the diagonal, will redirect the "stripes" in a way which may be more pleasing to you (see sweater 23, Diagonal Vest).

Variegated yarns can be fun to use in certain Fair Isle motifs, when contrasted with solid colors (see sweater 24, Icelandic Pullover).

Novelty yarns

Whether solid or multicolored, novelty yarns provide the designer with special challenges. Take care when using any highly textured yarn to avoid "busy" stitches or elaborate cables, which won't show up well. Slipped ribs on a reverse stockinette stitch background work well for some novelties (see sweater 2, Novelty Yarn Pullover).

A yarn with nubs will often work better in plain stockinette (see sweater 17, Silk and Linen Pullover). A stitch that is even slightly textured may hide the special feature that you worked hard to build in.

In a tweed yarn, a few accenting cables may be just enough to create an interesting design (see sweater 4, Tweed Pullover). In many cases, the simple act of paying careful attention to the overall shaping of the sweater may be enough to give your garment a distinctive look. Notice the simplicity of many of our garment shapes—the classics. They can effectively display many types of handspun yarns.

Special fibers

Angora: If used unblended, angora will be very furry and will not allow many stitch details to show. In our all-angora pullover (sweater

7), we decided to use a delicate eyelet stitch which adds a hint of texture. This sweater could be made entirely in stockinette, though, if you're a tentative knitter.

Plying angora with another fiber will reduce its fuzziness by half (see sweater 6, Angora and Silk Pullover). You can, as a result, use a greater variety of stitches. But keep in mind when you select stitches that the more you handle your knitted angora piece, the fluffier it will get.

Silk, linen, and ramie: These three fibers are not as resilient as wool. They need to be handled carefully by the designer. Make the ribbing at the lower edges and cuffs slightly tighter than you would make a wool ribbing, since in these fibers it will tend to stretch out of shape. Use a few less stitches and smaller needles. We solved this problem in the Camel and Silk Vest (sweater 10) by using the camel for ribbing; wool would serve the same purpose.

When deciding on the finished length of body and sleeves, remember that the weight of these fibers will cause the fabric to lengthen. A special stitch used throughout the garment can help counteract this tendency (see sweater 3, Linen Jacket).

Angora bunnies are fast on their feet.

Mohair: Handspun mohair feels and knits up differently than commercially spun mohair. The stitches are more rounded, instead of the usual oval shape. Several stitch patterns do not work well because of this. We can't predict which ones will work best, but regular ribbing produced gaps (a twisted rib cured the problem) and some laces looked awkward. Try out several variations on your swatch and engage your most critical eye (see sweater 19, Mohair Cardigan).

Specialty wools: There are many wools out there. Some offer quite distinctive qualities. Welsh Mountain fleece contains guard hairs which do not absorb dye as readily as the rest of the fibers; a design can take advantage of this (see sweater 18, Welsh Mountain Pullover). Cotswold, with its extra fiber length, takes well to color blending (see sweater 13, Cotswold Pullover). Merino has such a nice, soft, "creamy" feel to it that we could spin it forever; it's the fiber of choice for a luxurious wool sweater (see sweater 16, Merino Cardigan).

When you design a sweater, the number of color and texture combinations available to you is infinite. There are stripes, chevrons, solid ribbings used with a textured body, the alternation of variegated yarns with solids, and so much more.

Be sure to try carding fibers together. Hélène is now spinning a dyed fleece carded with natural white mohair. The result is a soft, fluffy, heathery yarn which is very pleasing.

The ideas keep popping up. They won't stop. We hope our designing notes for the individual sweaters will help you continue this process and come up with your own ideas.

The best advice we can offer is to experiment and to keep notes about what you like and dislike about the way each yarn knits up. And don't settle for less than you envision. If you don't like your first swatch, keep trying until you find the idea which will make your sweater someone's most prized possession!

Getting ready to knit

Making the right size

The word *gauge* has to be the most important word in a knitter's vocabulary. We strongly recommend that you become comfortable with making gauge swatches. They are essential when you work with commercial yarns, and even more important—if that's possible—for handspuns.

Without a proper understanding of how gauge affects your finished garment and how to achieve the correct gauge, it's difficult to make a knitted garment that fits. Every knitter has a particular "touch," also sometimes called tension, that is the result of the way the needles and yarn are held, and consequently determines how many stitches go into an inch of fabric. The difference in tension between knitters can vary a great deal when commercial yarns are used, and those strands are relatively uniform in thickness from skein to skein. Handspun yarn, even when carefully made to meet specifications, can easily vary from the "standard" we describe. Each handspun skein can also be slightly—or more noticeably—different from its neighbors. Therefore, gauge becomes even more important for the knitter who uses handspun.

The gauge principle is: *The number of stitches per inch divided into the total number of stitches in a row of knitting will give you the width in inches across the knitted piece.*

For example, you're working at a stitch gauge of 5 stitches per inch. You have 90 stitches on your needle. If you continue to knit, you will produce a piece of fabric 18 inches wide (90 divided by 5). If this is the front of a pullover, the fabric for the back would be the same size and your finished sweater would be 36 inches around.

Now let us imagine that your gauge, which you did *not* check by working a swatch at the beginning of your project, is actually 4.75 stitches per inch, but you are working a pattern which calls for 5 stitches per inch. Not a big difference? Your 90-stitch piece will measure 19 inches across (90 divided by 4.75), so your finished sweater will be 38 inches around—2 inches larger than you originally intended.

The sizes given for our sweaters reflect the finished dimensions of the garments, not the measurements of the person for whom they are being made.

The more "off-gauge" you are, the more "off-size" your knitting will be. While stitch gauge is used more often, row gauge (the number of rows in a vertical inch of fabric) is also important in raglan sleeves, circular yokes, and any patterns which require increases or decreases to be made at specific row intervals.

What can you do to guarantee that you are working at the correct gauge? Knit up a swatch at least 4 inches wide by 4 inches long, using the garment's main stitch (unless the instructions tell you to work a swatch in another stitch). Count the number of stitches and the number of rows in 2 inches and divide each of these numbers by 2 to get your stitch and row gauges. If you have fewer stitches per inch than are called for, try another swatch on smaller needles. If you have more stitches per inch than the pattern requires, make another swatch on larger needles.

Keep making swatches until you get it right. It sounds tedious and time-consuming, but why waste this wonderful yarn on a project that won't fit? In addition, you will want to check your tension regularly, either by measuring the width of the piece you are working on or by recalculating gauge from a small section of your actual knitting. Be satisfied—apply the gauge principle!

Determining yarn quantities

It is always nice to know in advance how much yarn you need to spin. We've spoken about this on page 8, and have given approximate quantities in each pattern. Extra yarn never hurts, and always comes in handy somewhere. Several of our sweaters came about because our basket of leftovers got too full—and the combinations became some of our favorite garments.

We hope you will leave this book determined to spin a brand new yarn to be used in a sweater of your own design. You'll want to know how much yarn you will need without having our notes to rely on, so here is the method we use to get some working numbers.

1. Spin enough fiber to give you 20 yards of yarn. (If you end up with more yardage, keep track of how much you have.) Make a 4" × 4" swatch in the main stitch for your garment, using the size

of needles which will produce the appropriate gauge. (This is testing time; work enough swatches to get the fabric right.) Measure how many yards you have *left* and subtract it from your original total to find out how many yards you have *used* in your swatch. In this example, let's say we have used 12 yards of yarn to make the swatch.

The rest of this process will be demonstrated through the example of a dropped-shoulder crew neck pullover. We have just discovered how many yards of yarn we need to make 16 square inches of fabric (4" × 4"). Now we need to know how many square inches of fabric are in our proposed garment.

2. Let's say we want to make a size 40 sweater (40" around the chest) with a body length of 25". To determine the area of the front and back, multiply 40 by 25 = 1000 square inches.

3. For each sleeve, multiply the width at the armhole (in this case, 19") by the sleeve's total length (say 20") = 380 square inches. Sleeves are shaped, so we subtract approximately 15% to account for this (380–57 = 323 square inches). There are two sleeves, so we'll need a total of 646 square inches.

4. Total body area (1000) plus total sleeve area (646) gives us 1646 square inches of fabric. Divide by 16 (the number of square inches in our swatch) to get about 103; multiply this by the yardage used in the swatch, 12, to get the yardage needed for the sweater = 1236 yards.

As long as your spinning is consistent, you can aim for 1236 yards of yarn. But extra never hurts. . . .

Knitting terms

We use common knitting abbreviations throughout the pattern section. Here are translations:

beg—beginning, begin.
ch—chain (crochet).
cn—cable needle.
dec—decrease.
dp needles—double-pointed needles.

Garter st—Garter stitch. When working back and forth, knit every row. When working on circular needles in rounds, knit one row and then purl one row, and repeat.

inc—increase.

K, k—knit.

K2tog—knit 2 stitches together.

P, p—purl.

p1b—purl 1 stitch through the back of the loop.

psso—pass the slipped stitch over the stitch just knitted.

rem—remaining.

Rev St st—reverse stockinette (stocking) stitch. Reverse directions for stockinette stitch. All purled rows will appear on right side of fabric, and all knitted rows will appear on wrong side.

sc—single crochet.

sl—slip a stitch.

sl 1 wyib—slip 1 stitch, keeping yarn in back of work.

slyf—specialized slip-stitch described in directions for sweater 23.

ssk—slip 2 stitches knitwise from left needle to right needle, one at a time; insert the left needle into the fronts of these stitches, from left to right, and knit them together. (NOTE: a one-step version of this process is illustrated in the section on finishing techniques.)

st, sts—stitch, stitches.

St st—stockinette (stocking) stitch. When working back and forth, knit one row and then purl the following row. When working in rounds on a circular needle, knit every row.

yo—bring working yarn to front between needles, up over right-hand needle, and to back; this makes a new stitch on the right-hand needle which can be worked on the next row.

Knitting techniques

There are a few shortcuts which will help you knit more easily and professionally.

Setting in dropped-shoulder sleeves: Hélène has found from experience that the armhole for dropped-shoulder sleeves tends to be smaller than it needs to be when it is measured in the usual way. Nor-

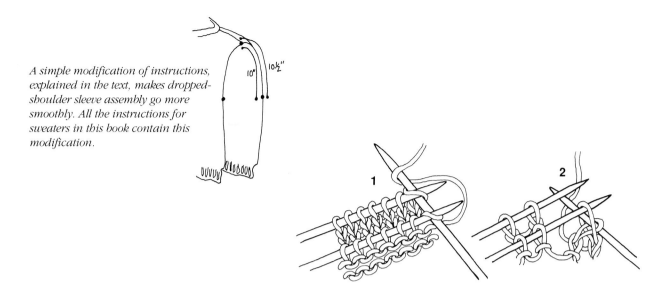

A simple modification of instructions, explained in the text, makes dropped-shoulder sleeve assembly go more smoothly. All the instructions for sweaters in this book contain this modification.

mal directions call for taking measurements, placing armhole markers, and sewing the sleeves between these markers.

To solve the problem, she knits the full length of the body, from ribbing to shoulder, and does not place underarm markers. When it is time to sew the sleeves into position, she measures down from the shoulder seam, adding $\frac{1}{2}$ to 1" to the armhold measurement given in the pattern. To get a 10" finished armhole, she places markers $10\frac{1}{2}$" from the shoulder seam on both the front and back. All the patterns in this book which require dropped-shoulder shaping allow for this extra space in their written instructions. On the drawings, however, the numbers given for the armhole depth and top of sleeve are finished measurements. This is a special hint for smoothly assembling dropped-shoulder sweaters; you may want to make the same adjustment on patterns from other sources, since most do not provide the additional ease for the seam.

Knitted seam: This is a technique for joining the top edges of two fabrics by knitting them together at the same time that you bind both edges off.

Seam assembly, stitched: To join the vertical or side edges of two fabrics, work with a yarn needle from the right side of the fabrics. Catch your needle under the horizontal bars of the stitches at the edges of the fabrics.

K2tog left (a one-step ssk): This is a neat trick to speed up your ssk decreases.

K2tog, left
Insert needle through the front of the first stitch and through the back of the second stitch; knit these two stitches together.

KNITTED SEAM
Step 1. With right sides of fabric held together and using a third needle, knit together the first stitches from both needles. At beginning of row only, repeat step 1 with the second stitches on both needles.

Step 2. Bind off the first stitch worked onto the right-hand needle by slipping it over the second stitch on that needle.

Repeat steps 1 and 2 across the row, until all stitches are bound off. Secure final stitch by drawing the working yarn through its loop.

SEAM ASSEMBLY, STITCHED
Place pieces side by wide, with right sides facing you. Insert needle under two rows at a time for sport- and worsted-weight yarns, or under every row for bulky-weight yarns, and take stitches on alternate sides, as shown. Pull yarn firmly as you go along.

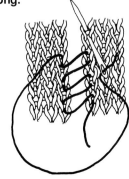

Our patterns are unusual, since they contain not only complete knitting instructions but also detailed information on preparing, dyeing, and spinning the fibers for the yarn. If you spin, we hope to introduce you to new territory and new ways of using your yarn. If you don't, perhaps we can reveal some of the mysteries of how yarns are made.

Since one of our goals is to increase the knitter's sensitivity to the range of available fibers, each pattern begins with a short account of our creative process along with details on the fiber type, its texture, our color decisions, and our choice of style.

When you select a pattern, begin by reading it through to be sure you understand the whole procedure.

The sizes indicated are only standards and won't necessarily fit everyone; when you produce a custom garment, you don't have to "put up" with a commercial size. Make necessary adjustments to the size of the garment (for example, length of front and back or of sleeves, armhole depth, or width at the back of the neck). Schematics are included to help you make these changes easily. Plan on increasing or decreasing your yarn quantities according to the changes you make (see page 29), "Determining Yarn Quantities").

Spin a sample quantity of yarn (see page 29). Then make a knitted sample and see if it works well at the required gauge and gives you a fabric which looks like the one in the close-up photo. Adjust your spinning if necessary (page 16). When you have the quantity of yarn you will need and are ready to knit, make a final gauge swatch and adjust the size of your needles until your gauge reading is perfect. At this point, you will be well prepared to execute your project successfully.

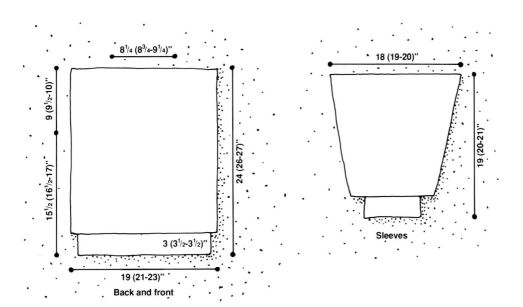

8¼ (8¾-9¼)"

9 (9½-10)"

15½ (16½-17)"

24 (26-27)"

3 (3½-3½)"

19 (21-23)"

Back and front

18 (19-20)"

19 (20-21)"

Sleeves

FIBER
type and source: Carded wool from Wilde Yarns.
characteristics: A medium-to-coarse grade of wool; fiber length is 3-5″.
preparation: Well-scoured wool was supplied in large batts, which were split to manageable size for spinning.
SPINNING TECHNIQUE: Supported long draw.
YARN
weight: Light bulky (4.25 stitches/inch).
yards per pound: 500.
number of plies: 2.
singles t.p.i.: 4-5.
plying t.p.i.: 3-4.

This simple style, in a light bulky weight, requires no dyeing and lets you concentrate on spinning technique and the traditional color patterns of the knitting.

We started with an all-around wool, in a medium grade, useful for many purposes. It was available in large batts and was well scoured and carded, so we could just start spinning. Our inspiration came from the colors of the fiber.

Similar fiber is available from the same source in both dyed and natural colors, but we were intrigued by a "pale yellow" natural shade and chose to work in three natural colors in order not to lose the special quality of that color. Spinners soon become aware that not all white wool is *white*. Using this softly-yellowed wool as the main color allowed us to work with more muted contrasts than we would have had with a pure white.

Our trial run indicated that the fibers felt a little coarse but were well prepared and drew out nicely. The slight coarseness of the wool suggested an outdoor garment, and the natural colors "asked" to be worked into a traditional Fair Isle pattern. We needed a smooth yarn so the motifs would not be distorted.

We updated our Fair Isle's style by using a boatneck instead of one of the traditional necklines. The boatneck also allowed us to complete the pattern without breaking into the design for neckline shaping—and for the same reason, we selected a dropped shoulder. The ribbing at the top and bottom of the body sections frames the center design, still without interrupting the layout of the pattern—lots easier than keeping track of colors when you're shaping other types of necklines and shoulders. In addition, the ribbing fabric (worked with one strand of yarn) is less bulky than the body fabric (where the unused colors are carried behind the work). This puts the warmth where it's needed.

Made with a light bulky weight yarn at 4.25 stitches per inch, this design works up reasonably fast. The style is appropriate for men or women. Although we like our naturals, we'd also love to see this worked with a black background, and patterns of colors like fuchsia and turquoise.

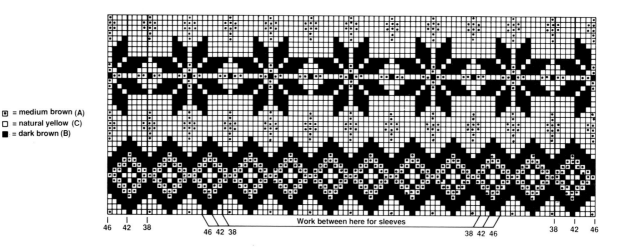

= medium brown (A)
= natural yellow (C)
= dark brown (B)

Work between here for sleeves

46 42 38   46 42 38   38 42 46   38 42 46

KNITTING INSTRUCTIONS

Instructions are for finished size 38". Changes for sizes 42" and 46" are in parentheses.

Materials: Wilde Yarns carded wool, spun to light bulky weight: 13 (14-15^1/$_2$) ounces or 405 (440-480) yards medium brown (A), 10^1/$_2$ (11^1/$_4$-12^1/$_4$) ounces or 325 (350-380) yards dark brown (B), 13 (14-15^1/$_4$) ounces or 400 (435-475) yards natural yellow. One pair each size 7 and 10 needles or size to obtain correct gauge.

Gauge: In Color pattern with size 10 needles, 4.25 sts and 4 rows = 1".

Back: With smaller needles and A, cast on 75 (83-91) sts. Work in ribbing as follows: Row 1: K1, *p1, k1. Row 2: P1, *k1, p1. Repeat these 2 rows until 3 (3^1/$_2$-3^1/$_2$)" from beginning, inc 6 sts evenly in last row—81 (89-97) sts. With larger needles, work in St st following chart repeating these 38 rows 2 times. Right side facing, k across with A only, then continue working in ribbing as for lower edge until 24 (26-27)" from beginning. For shoulders, work across 23 (26-29) sts and leave on holder, firmly bind off next 35 (37-39) sts, work to end of row and leave these 23 (26-29) sts on holder.

Front: Work as for back.

Sleeves: With smaller needles and A, cast on 35 (37-39) sts. Work in ribbing as for back for 3", inc 16 (18-20) sts evenly in last row—51 (55-59) sts. Then, with larger needles, work in St st following chart and inc 1 st each end every 1 (1^1/$_4$-1^1/$_3$)" 13 times working new sts in established Color pattern. Work even on obtained 77 (81-85) sts until 19 (20-21)" from beginning. Bind off all sts.

Finishing: Join shoulder seams using the knitted seam method. Then, measure 9^1/$_2$ (10-10^1/$_2$)" on each side of shoulder seams and place markers on armhole edges. Set in sleeves between markers stretching slightly to fit. Sew underarm and side seams.

36

Spin wool singles with one strand of cotton.

Apply the second strand of cotton in a plying process to achieve the criss-cross effect.

Fiber

type and source: Carded wool from Wilde Yarns; 4 ounces size 20/2 weaving cotton (from any weaving supplier).

characteristics: A medium-to-coarse grade of wool; fiber length is 3-5".

preparation: Well-scoured wool was supplied in large batts, which were split to manageable size for spinning.

SPINNING TECHNIQUE: Supported long draw. As the wool was spun, one strand of weaving cotton was held next to the fibers as they are drawn out. Take care to maintain a consistent 4 t.p.i. so that the intended criss-cross effect will occur when the second strand of cotton is plied on.

YARN

weight: Bulky (4 stitches/inch in rib).

yards per pound: 635.

number of plies: 2.

singles t.p.i.: 4.

plying t.p.i.: 2.

Beginning with the same commercially-carded, medium-grade wool as we used for our Fair Isle pullover, we spun the yarn and then dyed it. We wanted to produce a novelty yarn, something a little different. To "hold" a textured effect and work well for a sweater of this type, the wool chosen must not be too fine (the texture crushes out) or too coarse (the garment can become very rough, and use of a coarse yarn is limited to things like lined jackets).

We were looking for a bulky yarn which was lofty, not heavy, and obtained it by combining commercial cotton with the wool. While the wool singles were spun, we held a strand of lightweight weaving cotton alongside the fibers as we drafted. This two-element strand was then plied with another strand of lightweight weaving cotton. If you count the twists per inch in both singles and plying, the two cotton strands will make a cross-pattern around the wool (see notes on spinning technique).

We used black cotton for our fine yarn and then dyed the completed yarn a rich, reddish purple. The color of the black cotton was unaffected by the dyebath. This is because animal and vegetable fibers require different types of dye; dye that colors wool does not affect cotton. You can change to a different dye color, but it should be light enough to allow the contrasting cotton to show. Consider the use of a different color of thread as well, but test to see what effect your dye will have on it. You could also get the effect of this yarn by starting with one of the commercially dyed colors in which this wool is available.

We decided to make a raglan-sleeve outdoor pullover, with a special rib stitch and a cable. The raglan sleeves fit comfortably, and don't restrict the arm movements of outdoor activities. Full-fashioned shaping on the raglan allowed us to run the rib up the sleeve without interruption.

The trick when using pattern stitches with a novelty yarn is in finding an appropriate combination. We made a number of swatches before we found a cable pattern which works with this yarn. Both the cable and the rib incorporate slipped stitches, which are worked only on every other row. This elongates those stitches, makes them stand

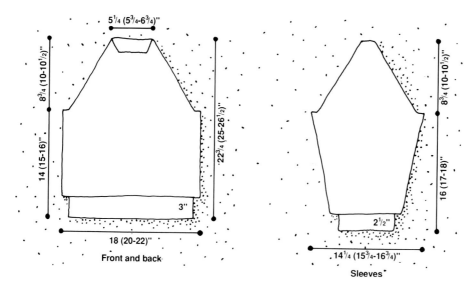

Front and back

Sleeves

up better, and allows them to show up against the texture of the yarn. Working on a base of reverse stockinette also permits the stitch patterns to be more evident. Oddly enough, because of the dominance of the wool strand in this yarn, it feels like a single-ply yarn when you knit it.

KNITTING INSTRUCTIONS

Instructions are for finished size 36". Changes for sizes 40" and 44" are in parentheses.

Materials: Wilde Yarns carded wool and thread, spun to bulky weight: $16\frac{3}{4}$ (20-$23\frac{1}{4}$) ounces or 665 (795-925) yards. One each 24" size 7 and 9 circular needle or size to obtain correct gauge. One 16" and one 29" size 9 circular needle, one set size 7 double-pointed needles (dp needles). Four markers.

Gauge: In Rib pattern with size 9 needle, 4 sts and 5.5 rows = 1".

Stitches Used: *Rib stitch—Rnd 1:* *K1, p3; rep from *, end k1. *Rnd 2:* *Sl 1 with yarn in back (wyib), p3; rep from *, end sl 1 wyib. Repeat these 2 rnds for pattern. *Cable stitch—Rnd 1:* P3, k1, p2, k1, p3. *Rnds 2 & 3:* P3, sl 1 wyib, p2, sl 1 wyib, p3. *Rnd 4:* P1, slip next 2 purl sts, drop next st off needle to front of work, slip the 2 purl sts back to left-hand needle, pick up dropped st and knit it, p4. Drop next st off needle to front of work, p2, pick up dropped st and knit it, p1. *Rnds 5, 6, & 7:* P1, k1, p6, k1, p1. *Rnds 8 & 9:* P1, sl 1 wyib, p6, sl 1 wyib, p1. *Rnd 10:* P1, drop next st off needle to front of work, p2, pick up dropped st and knit it, p2, slip the next 2 purl sts to right-hand needle, drop next st off needle to front of work, slip the same 2 purl sts back to left-hand needle, pick up dropped st and knit it, p3. *Rnds 11, 12, & 13:* As rnds 1, 2, & 3. *Rnd 14:* P3, drop next st off needle to front of work, slip 2 purl sts, drop next st off needle to front, then holding the 2 purl sts on right-hand needle, pick up the first dropped st onto left-hand needle, then slip the 2 purl sts back to left-hand needle, then pick up the 2nd dropped st and return it to left-hand needle, then k1, p2, k1, p3. Repeat these 14 rnds for pattern.

DYEING

dye type and source: Acid dyes. We used Craftsman's acid dyes from The Ruggery.

process: We dyed the yarn with three parts magenta and one part violet. Weigh the dry yarn, then let it soak in a pan of hot tap water while you prepare the dyebath. In a stainless steel or enamel pan on the stove, mix $\frac{1}{2}$ cup of white vinegar per pound of dry yarn weight with enough water to let the yarn float loosely. Wearing rubber gloves, mix a little dye powder with a few drops of water in a glass measuring cup, then add some of this paste to the pot of vinegar water. Mix the dye powders as you like to get the color you want—$\frac{3}{4}$ teaspoon magenta and $\frac{1}{4}$ teaspoon violet made our color, and then we added the paste a little at a time to
(continued)

This bulky yarn incorporates two strands of fine commercial cotton and was dyed after it was spun; the knitting pattern was designed to complement, rather than compete with, the yarn.

Note: Body is worked in one piece to armholes. Then, sleeves are worked and added on, and yoke is worked in one piece to neck. You may want to use markers between motifs.

Body: With smaller circular needle, cast on 130 (146-162) sts. Place marker at beginning of rnd and work around in k1, p1 rib taking care not to twist first rnd, for 2½", inc 14 sts evenly in last rnd—144 (160-176) sts. Then, with larger circular needle, begin at marker, p2, Rib st on 21 (25-29) sts, Cable st on 10 sts, p1, Rib st on 5 sts, p1, Cable st on 10 sts, Rib st on 45 (53-61) sts, Cable st on 10 sts, p1, Rib st on 5 sts, p1, Cable st on 10 sts, Rib st on 21 (25-29) sts, p1. Work as established until 14 (15-16)" from beginning or desired length to underarms. Bind off 5 sts at beginning of next rnd, work across 63 (71-79) sts and leave on holder, bind off next 9 sts, work across 63 (71-79) sts and leave on holder, bind off last 4 sts. Keep note of which Cable st rnd you end on for matching with sleeves.

Sleeves: With dp needles, cast on 32 (34-36) sts. Place marker at beginning of rnd and work around in k1, p1 rib for 3", inc 19 (17-19) sts evenly in last rnd—51 (51-55) sts. Then, beginning at marker, with 16" larger circular needle, work around as follows: P 0 (0-2) sts, Rib st on 21 sts, Cable st on 10 sts, Rib st on 20 (20-21) sts omitting last st on Rib st pattern for sizes 36 and 40, and ending with p1 for size 44. Work as established, inc 1 st each side of marker at underarm every 3½ (2¼-2⅓)" 3 (6-6) times working new sts in Rib st. Work even on obtained 57 (63-67) sts until approximately 16 (17-18)" from beginning ending with same Cable rnd as for body. Bind off 5 sts at beg of next rnd, work to last 4 sts, bind off these 4 sts—48 (54-58) sts.

Yoke: With 29" larger circular needle, work across in pattern as follows: From body holders, work across first 63 (71-79) sts, place marker, then across 48 (54-58) sts from first sleeve holder, place marker, across second 63 (71-79) sts from body holders, place marker, then across 48 (54-58) sts from second sleeve holder, place marker—222 (250-274) sts. To shape raglan, work as follows: After each marker, k1, ssk, work to 3 sts before next marker, k2 tog, k1. Work this decrease rnd every 3 rnds 6 times, then every 2 rnds 15 (18-20) times. AT THE SAME TIME, at 6 (7-7¾)" above armhole, leave center 11 (13-17) sts of front panel on holder. Then, work back and forth keeping armhole decreases as established and decreasing 1 st at neck edges every right side row 3 times.

get the depth of color we wanted. To check the color, scoop out a little of the mixed dyebath into another glass measuring cup and hold it up to the light. It's better to have the dye solution a little too weak than a little too strong because it is always easier to add more dye than to remove color. This visual color test is not totally accurate because certain dyes will not color the wool until a certain temperature (usually boiling) is reached. When the dye looks good, lift your wet yarn out of the water and plunge it all at once into the dyepot. Turn on the stove to high and swish the yarn around gently while it heats to simmer. When the yarn is the color you want, or when the dye water looks clear, remove the yarn. If this took less than ½ hour in steaming heat, then add the same amount of vinegar to a pot of clear water, and heat the dyed yarn in that for ½ hour to finish setting the dye. Rinse well but do not felt the yarn by too much handling or by abrupt changes of water temperature.

Neckband: Once raglan decreases are completed, work neckband as follows: With dp needles, work across 37 (39-43) sts left on needle, pick up and k 8 sts on side of neck, work across 11 (13-17) sts from front holder, pick up and k 8 sts on side of neck. Work around in k1, p1 rib on these 64 (68-76) sts for 2". Bind off all sts loosely in rib.

Finishing: Fold band in half to inside and slip stitch loosely in place. Sew underarm seams.

FIBER

type and source: Dyed flax roving from Euroflax, in pink and parma (a lilac color), 1 pound of each (we had some of the parma left over).

characteristics: Tow linen; fiber length varies widely, between 1″ and 6″.

preparation: This completely prepared fiber was pulled to a manageable size for spinning. Some spinners might choose to work from a folded length, if they are comfortable with that technique.

SPINNING TECHNIQUE: Sliding long draw. The forward hand smoothed the fiber into place.

YARN

weight: Worsted (4.75 stitches/inch in pattern).

yards per pound: 620.

number of plies: 2 (1 pink, 1 parma).

singles t.p.i.: 6.

plying t.p.i.: 3.

Commercially processed and dyed flax was spun in two colors, which we plied together and made into a jacket which combines a diagonal chevron stitch and garter stitch.

This is the only fiber we used which was commercially dyed, although you could adapt many of our designs for use with the beautiful dyed fibers that are now available. This flax is available in a wide range of colors, and the resulting yarn is machine washable and dryable. Once we had the linen in hand, it said "jacket." Then we needed to design an appropriate yarn.

Despite the numerous existing possibilities, we wanted to make a simple, feminine jacket in a color *between* the available colors. When you're a spinner you can suit yourself ! The easiest way to make an intermediate color is to select two existing shades, spin one-color singles, and ply them together. If the two colors you pick are very different, you'll end up with a salt-and-pepper yarn (like that used in "ragg" socks). With two closely related colors, however, you'll get a subtle blend like the one in this sweater. A single-color yarn would work well in this design, and many other color combinations could be derived from the supplier's selection. Because linen feels "dressy" to us, we made our yarn smooth so we could freely use textured stitches.

In the introduction, we spoke about differences in wool grades. The same distinctions occur in plant fibers, although many contemporary handspinners are not yet familiar enough with non-wool fibers to realize this fully. When spinning this flax, we noticed a large difference in texture between the two batches. The pink felt coarser and didn't go quite as far as the lilac for the same weight of fiber. We did run out of yarn and had to make more (when this happens to you, don't panic). We filled out with a slightly different dyelot, and used skeins alternately when we knit so the color change isn't apparent in the finished garment.

There are many ways to design a jacket, but this short, carefully detailed version would be a versatile addition to many wardrobes. The front closure features crocheted button loops. The sleeves are full both above the cuffs and at the shoulders, but not so full that they're puffed.

Linen requires different design considerations than wool, because it is less elastic, heavier, and tends to "grow" (or stretch out of shape when worn). The stitches we selected needed to take this into ac-

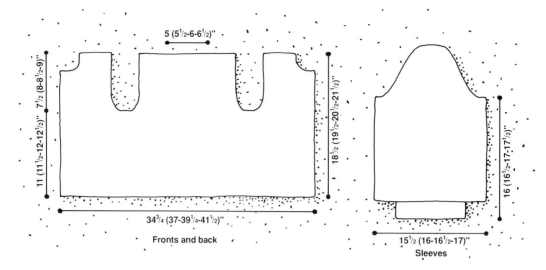

5 (5½-6-6½)"

11 (11½-12-12½)" 7½ (8-8½-9)"

18½ (19½-20½-21½)"

34¾ (37-39¼-41½)"

Fronts and back

16 (16½-17-17½)"

15½ (16-16½-17)"

Sleeves

count. The chevron motif places the stitches on the diagonal, giving the fabric body and counteracting the natural gravitational pull. The chevron gives the fabric a zigzag shape which enhances the bottom edge, but its use throughout the sweater would have complicated shoulder shaping, so we switched to garter stitch for the yoke. This gave us a smooth surface. The two stitch patterns have different gauges, so we needed to decrease stitches when we changed patterns in order to keep the fabric at the proper width. The cuff of the sleeve repeats the chevron pattern, while the remainder of the sleeve is in garter stitch so the shaping is easy.

The attention we have paid to the way this sweater drapes makes the style appropriate for a number of yarns with less elasticity than wool, including silk, ramie, and cotton, as well as the linen shown.

KNITTING INSTRUCTIONS

Instructions for finished size 34¾". Changes for 37", 39¼", and 41½" are in parentheses.

Materials: Euroflax dyed roving, spun to worsted weight: 23 (25½-27¾-30¼) ounces or 895 (990-1075-1170) yards linen. One each 29" size 4 and 6 circular needle or size to obtain correct gauge. Seven ½" buttons. One size F crochet hook.

Gauge: In Pattern st with size 6 needle, 19 sts = 4". In Garter st with size 4 needle, 16 sts and 33 rows = 4".

Stitches Used: *Pattern stitch—Row 1 (wrong side):* K. *Rows 2, 4, 6, & 8:* *K2 tog, k2, k in front and back of next 2 sts, k3, ssk; repeat from *. *Rows 3, 5, & 7:* Purl. Repeat these 8 rows for pattern.

Note: Body is worked in one piece to armholes.

Body: With smaller needle, cast on 140 (150-160-170) sts. Work in Garter st for 5 rows, inc 25 (26-27-28) sts evenly in last row—165 (176-187-198) sts. Then, with wrong side facing and larger needle, work in Pattern st. Work as established until approximately 11 (11½-12-12½)" from beginning, ending with row 8 of Pattern st. With smaller needle, continue in Garter st, evenly decreasing 25 (28-29-32) sts in second row—140 (148-158-166) sts. Work even until you have worked ½" in Garter st.

Right Front Yoke: With right side facing and working in Garter st for rest of yoke, work across 31 (33-35-37) sts and leave remaining sts on holder. Then, working on this side only, dec 1 st at armhole edge every other row 5 times. Work even on remaining 26 (28-30-32) sts until 5 ($5^{1}/_{2}$-6-$6^{1}/_{2}$)" above armhole. Bind off 6 (7-7-8) sts at beginning of next right side row (neck edge), then dec 1 st at same edge every other row 4 times. Work even on remaining 16 (17-19-20) sts until $7^{1}/_{2}$ (8-$8^{1}/_{2}$-9)" above armhole. Leave sts on holder.

Back Yoke: Bind off first 8 sts from holder, work on next 62 (66-72-76) sts, and leave remaining sts on holder. Then, working on these sts only, dec 1 st each end every other row 5 times. Work even on remaining 52 (56-62-66) sts until $7^{1}/_{2}$ (8-$8^{1}/_{2}$-9)" above armhole bind-off row. Right side facing, work across 16 (17-19-20) sts and leave on holder, bind off center 20 (22-24-26) sts, work on remaining sts and leave on holder.

Left Front Yoke: Bind off first 8 sts from holder and work on remaining 31 (33-35-37) sts as for right front yoke, reversing armhole and neck shapings.

Sleeves: With smaller needle, cast on 44 (44-55-55) sts. Work back and forth in Garter st for 5 rows; then with larger needles, work in Pattern st for 1 repeat. With smaller needles, continue working in Garter st, inc 18 (20-11-13) sts evenly in second row—62 (64-66-68) sts. Work even for rest of sleeve. Shape armholes and cap: At 16 ($16^{1}/_{2}$-17-$17^{1}/_{2}$)" from beginning or desired length to underarm. (Remember that a sleeve knitted in this yarn will tend to "grow.") Bind off 4 sts at beg of next 2 rows, then dec 1 st each end every 4th row 12 times, then every other row until 24 sts remain. Bind off 4 sts at beg of next 4 rows. Bind off remaining 8 sts. Sew underarm sleeve seams.

Finishing: Join shoulder seams using the knitted seam method. Then, with crochet hook, work 3 rows single crochet on left front opening. Break yarn. Attach yarn at lower edge of right front and work 1 row single crochet evenly spacing 7 "chain-2" buttonloops along edge positioning first loop 1" from lower edge and top loop $^{1}/_{4}$" from top edge. Work 3 sc in corner, work around neck opening, work 3 sc in left top corner, then work down to lower edge (this will make a fourth single crochet row on left front opening). Break yarn. Sew buttons opposite buttonloops. Set in sleeves, gathering slightly to fit into armhole openings.

4 TWEED PULLOVER

Local fleeces can be treasures. The wool for this sweater came from Anne Gass's flock; in her Moose Crossing breeding program she crosses Corriedale, Romney, and Lincoln with the goal of achieving long, shiny, soft fibers. We used a hogget fleece, which is from the animal's first shearing. This fleece was quite long (7-8") and felt extremely fine and soft. Hogget fleece is characteristically longer, finer, and oilier than the adult fleece from the same animal will be. This sheep's wool was naturally dark brown; we selected the color because it was unusual and it offered a challenge for designing our yarn. Both color and style are suitable for men or women.

There were many appropriate ways in which we could have prepared and spun this fleece. Although we prefer working with clean fleece, this wool "felt" as though it "wanted" to be spun in the grease. However, in order to successfully spin without washing, you need to work with a freshly shorn fleece and we weren't able to get to this one in time. The fleece would also have been nice to prepare carefully with wool combs, for pure worsted spinning, but wool combs are expensive and most handspinners are not yet proficient in their use. So we did scour it and then prepared it on a drum carder.

Because of the combined length and fineness, the wool would have been appropriate spun at many different weights, from fine to heavy. We chose a light bulky weight, suitable for a wear-everywhere sweater.

We had a tweed yarn in mind for this collection, and the dark brown seemed an ideal background color. The flecks of contrasting color were added by carding in "garnetted" bits of yarn—little snips of spun yarn. To make the yarn we garnetted, we took scraps of red, yellow, green, and blue fleece. We divided our supply of each color in half, and spun the colors onto two bobbins in the same sequence, beginning with red and ending with blue. We then plied these two strands together; the colors generally aligned red-to-red, and so forth, but the transitions between colors included two-color plyings for short distances. We made a two-yard skein of this yarn, tied it, and snipped 1/4" lengths of fiber.

Before combining the colors with the brown wool, we completely carded the fleece and laid the batts out on a large space. We added

FIBER

type and source: Raw crossbred wool from Anne Gass of Moose Crossing. Scraps of hand-dyed, handspun wool yarn (a total of two ounces) in bright red, yellow, blue, and green.

characteristics: A fine wool, 5-6 crimps per inch; fiber length is 7-8″.

preparation: The wool was lightly picked and then scoured. The dry fiber was teased completely and carded on a drum carder. Quarter-inch garnets were added to each batt, which was then carded twice more. Batts were pulled to a manageable size for spinning.

SPINNING TECHNIQUE: Supported long draw.

YARN

weight: Light bulky (4.25 stitches/inch).

yards per pound: 560.

number of plies: 2.

singles t.p.i.: 4-5.

plying t.p.i.: 3.

A delightful, locally grown fleece and hand-dyed wool scraps combine in a sweater perfect for town or country.

an even amount of the snipped yarn to each batt, scattering the variety of colors throughout.

How much carding was enough to incorporate the garnetted fibers without losing their impact? We experimented. After one carding, the color touches were too sharp. Two cardings softened their ends. Since three cardings homogenized the wool, we worked the garnets into our fleece with only two cardings. When the finished yarn was washed, the garnetted fibers were also more securely incorporated.

Other colors could be used, both in the base fleece and in the garnetting yarns. You could combine a gray fleece with either lavenders and blues or with "Arizona" colors, or a white fleece with the crayon colors we used or with dark earth tones. A dressier version could be made in Merino, with bits of angora or silk.

We wanted a basic sweater which could be worn under many circumstances. Because the yarn was so highly textured, we needed a subdued design. We decided to make the sweater's construction interesting, though, and developed a different approach to the conventional crew-neck pullover. By working the sleeves from cuff-to-cuff, with a saddle-type shoulder, we could carry a cable horizontally across the shoulder area. We picked up and knit the body after the sleeve-and-yoke area was complete. The small cables and a widely spaced garter-stitch ridge keep the fabric interesting without overburdening the design.

KNITTING INSTRUCTIONS

Instructions are for finished size 36". Changes for sizes 39", 42", and 45" are in parentheses.

Materials: Anne Gass's raw wool, with garnets, spun to light bulky weight: 24 (28-31½-36) ounces or 840 (980-1105-1260) yards. One pair each size 4 and 6 needles, or size to obtain correct gauge. One 16" size 4 circular needle. One cable needle (cn).

Gauge: In St st with size 6 needles, 4.25 sts=1".

Stitches Used: *Ridged stitch—Row 1 and all right-side rows:* K. *Rows 2, 4, & 6:* P. *Row 8:* K. Repeat these 8 rows for pattern. *Cable (worked on 8 sts)— Rows 1 & 3:* P2, k4, p2. *Row 2 and all wrong side rows:* K2, p4, k2. *Row 5:* P2, sl 2 to cn, hold in front, k2, k2 from cn, p2. *Row 7:* As row 1. *Row 8:* As row 2. Repeat these 8 rows for pattern.

Note: Sleeves are worked from cuff to cuff, then front and back are worked down from the yoke.

Right Sleeve: With smaller needles, cast on 35 (37-39-41) sts. Work as follows: Row 1: K1, *p1, k1; rep from *. Row 2: P1, *k1, p1; rep from *. Work these 2 rows until 3" from beg, inc 11 (13-15-17) sts evenly in last row—46 (50-54-58) sts. Then, with larger needles, work across as follows: Work Ridged st on 11 (12-14-15) sts, Cable on 8 sts, Ridged st on center 8 (10-10-12) sts, Cable on 8 sts, Ridged st on 11 (12-14-15) sts. Work as established, inc 1 st each end every 1" 12 (14-16-17) times working new sts in Ridged st— 70 (78-86-92) sts. Work even until 17$\frac{1}{2}$ (18$\frac{1}{2}$-19$\frac{1}{2}$-20$\frac{1}{2}$)" from beg.

Yoke: Bind off 23 (26-30-32) sts at beg of next 2 rows. Work even in established pattern on remaining 24 (26-26-28) sts for 6 (6$\frac{1}{2}$-6$\frac{3}{4}$-7$\frac{1}{4}$)". Next wrong-side row, for back, work across 12 (13-13-14) sts, leave remaining sts on holder. Working on this side only, work even for 6 (6$\frac{1}{2}$-7$\frac{1}{2}$-8)" ending ready to work a right-side row. Leave sts on holder. To complete front, wrong-side facing, leave first 4 (5-5-6) sts on holder for side of neck, placing a marker at first st to mark shoulder line, then work even on remaining 8 sts until same length as back. Right-side facing, work across 8 sts, cast on 4 (5-5-6) sts, work across 12 (13-13-14) sts from back holder—24 (26-26-28) sts. Work even for 6 (6$\frac{1}{2}$-6$\frac{3}{4}$-7$\frac{1}{4}$)" more.

Left Sleeve: Cast on 23 (26-30-32) sts at beg of next 2 rows—70 (78-86-92) sts. Work down reversing shaping of first sleeve, changing needle size when ready to work cuff. Once complete, bind off using larger needle.

Front: On edge of front yoke, right side facing and using larger needles, pick up and k 77 (83-90-96) sts. Work in Ridged st beginning with row 8 of pattern and work down until 8$\frac{1}{2}$ (9$\frac{1}{2}$-10$\frac{1}{2}$-11)" from shoulder line marker, place marker each end for armholes. Work even in established pattern for 11$\frac{1}{2}$ (12-12$\frac{1}{2}$-13)" more, evenly decreasing 8 (8-9-9) sts in last row—69 (75-

81-87) sts. Then, with smaller needles, work in rib as for sleeve cuffs for 3".
Using larger needle, bind off all sts.

Back: Work as for front.

Neckband: With circular needle, attach yarn at left edge of neck, pick up
and k 4 (5-5-6) sts on side of neck, pick up and k 26 (28-32-35) sts on front
edge of neck, work across 4 (5-5-6) sts from holder, pick up and k 26 (28-32-
35) sts on back edge of neck. Work around in k1, p1 rib on these 60 (66-74-
82) sts for 1". Bind off in rib.

Finishing: Sew top of sleeves to side of front and back between markers
stretching slightly to fit. Sew underarm and side seams.

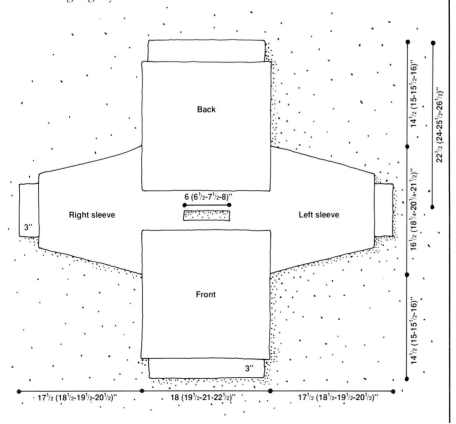

FIBER

type and source: Raw Maine island fleece from Wildwood.

characteristics: A medium-grade wool; fiber length is 4-6″.

preparation: The wool was picked, scoured, and dyed; then it was completely teased, carded, and finally pulled to a manageable size for spinning.

DYEING

dye type and source: Telana dye from Cerulean Blue, scarlet. These dyes were formerly called Lanaset dyes—it's the same dye, just a change of name. When you order the Telana dye, also order the 56% acetic acid, glauber's salt, albegel set, sodium acetate, and short range pH paper that you will need. You will also need a scale that can weigh very small amounts, such as a postage scale.

process: After the wool is picked and scoured, dry it thoroughly. Weigh the dry wool, since all chemical and dye amounts are based on a percentage of the dry fiber weight. The weight of the dry fiber is called weight of fiber, or WOF. Put on your rubber gloves. Into a stainless steel or enamel dyepot measure 9½ quarts of hot tap water for each pound of fiber weight. To this dyepot, add 4 teaspoons of 56% acetic acid per pound of wool; 1.6 ounces of glauber's salt; 1 teaspoon of albegel set; and .64 ounces

(continued)

Hélène wanted to work with a yarn which was round enough to give real distinction to an all-over textured stitch pattern, in the style of the traditional Guernsey sweaters. Rachael suggested a three-ply, which required a fleece that could be spun finely.

Rachael had spun Maine island fleece before, and found it to be a lovely medium-grade clean fleece, soft and with medium-to-long fibers. Although it is fine, it is not extremely crimpy and can therefore be spun into a smooth, tight yarn. While beginners find Maine island fleeces easy to spin, experienced spinners appreciate their beautiful whiteness and their ability to take pastel dyes well without distorting the colors. Of course, they also make outstanding undyed yarns.

The idea was to produce a contemporary sweater based on the idea of the traditional Guernsey, updating the styling and choosing the least common of the traditional colors—red. Many more of the old sweaters are in navy and natural. Lighter and brighter colors help textured stitch patterns show up in the fabric, as does a fleece with some luster.

All choices about dyeing were made to promote a rich, even color which would not detract from the sweater's styling and texture. Telana dyes give fantastic results—solid color with no streaking—but they require lots of attention to time, temperature, and quantities of dye and fiber. Litmus paper is used to test the dyebath's acidity level. This type of dye project is not one to undertake when interruptions are expected—save it for a calm day!

Dyeing your own fibers is always a little unpredictable. Part of learning to dye is learning to accept—and perhaps even enjoy—this fact, and running test batches. Dye powders kept in storage do not always give predictable results. Shelf-life information is usually supplied with the dyes; after the "expiration" date, the dyes still work but you may not get the intensity or shade of color you expect. In addition, two different fleeces will often "take" the same dye differently.

While we expected that a 1% dyebath of straight Telana scarlet would give us red, it produced a gorgeous rose color from our first dyebath. Wonderful, but not what we had in mind! We went back to the dyes, mixed a 3% bath of the same color, and produced the perfect red.

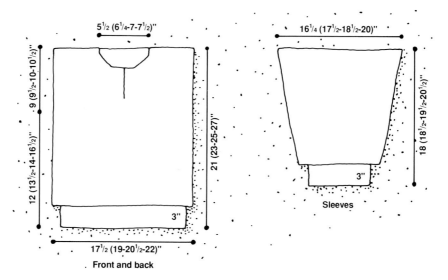

5½ (6¼-7-7½)"

9 (9½-10-10½)"

12 (13½-14-16½)"

21 (23-25-27)"

17½ (19-20½-22)"

3"

Front and back

16¼ (17½-18½-20)"

18 (18½-19½-20½)"

3"

Sleeves

of sodium acetate. With the pH paper, test for acidity between 4.5 and 5.0. If the pH is lower than 5.0, the solution is too acid, so add a bit of sodium acetate till the right number is reached. If the solution tests higher than 4.5 it is too alkaline, so add a little acetic acid and test again. Add dye after making it into a wet paste in a glass measuring cup. We used a 3% solution of scarlet dye, which means the dry dye powder weighed 3% of the weight of the dry fiber (.48 ounce/pound). Add wet, presoaked fiber and stir occasionally over a 10 minute period while holding the temperature at 120° F. Then slowly heat the dyebath to 212° F, taking 45 to 50 minutes for this heat rise. Stir every 10 minutes while the heat rises. Then hold the temperature at 212° F for an additional 20 to 30 minutes. Remove the fiber

(continued)

A three-ply yarn made from precisely dyed fiber requires more effort, but when the result is a sweater of this quality you won't hesitate.

We departed from the traditional Guernsey styling with the placket-and-collar neckline, the vertical (rather than horizontal) orientation of the stitch pattern, and the extension of cables into the ribbing area at the lower edges and collar. We kept the dropped-shoulder shaping of the original design.

KNITTING INSTRUCTIONS

Instructions are for finished size 35". Changes for sizes 38", 41", and 44" are in parentheses.

Materials: Wildwood's Maine island fleece, spun to worsted weight: 17¾ (20½-23½-27) ounces or 965 (1115-1280-1465) yards wool. One pair each size 4 and 6 needles or size to obtain correct gauge. One 16" size 6 circular needle, one cable needle (cn). Two buttons, ½".

Gauge: In St st with size 6 needle, 5 sts = 1".

Stitches Used: *Stockinette stitch. Reverse Stockinette stitch. Garter stitch. Cable (worked on 4 sts)—Rows 1 & 3: K4. Row 2 and all wrong side rows: P4. Row 5: Sl 2 to cn, hold in front, k2, k2 from cn. Row 6: As row 2. Repeat these 6 rows for pattern. Pattern stitch—Rows 1 & 3: K. Row 2 and all wrong-side rows: P. Rows 5 & 7: K2, *p3, k2; rep from *. Row 8: As row 2. Repeat these 8 rows for pattern.*

Back: With smaller needles, cast on 78 (86-94-102) sts. Size 35: Row 1: P2, *Cable on 4 sts, p2, k2, p2; rep from *, end with Cable on 4 sts, p2. Size 38: Row 1: P2, k2, p2, work from * on size 35 to end of row. Size 41: Row 1: (p2, k2) 2 times, p2, work from * on size 35 to last 4 sts, k2, p2. Size 44: P2, (k2, p2) 3 times, work from * on size 35 to last 8 sts, (k2, p2) 2 times. Row 2 for all sizes: K on k, p on p. Work as established for 3", inc 11 (11-9-9) sts evenly in last row as follows: Inc 1 st before 1st Cable for sizes 35 and 38 only, 3 sts between 1st and 3rd Cable, 3 sts between 3rd and 6th Cable, 3 sts between 6th and 8th Cable, 1 st at end of row for sizes 35 and 38 only—89 (97-103-111) sts. With larger needles, work across as follows: St st on 2 (6-9-13) sts, Rev St st on 1 st, Cable on 4 sts, Rev St st on 1 st, chart on 17 sts, Rev St st on 1 st, Cable on 4 sts, Rev St st on 1 st, Pattern st on center 27 sts, Rev St st on 1 st, Cable on 4 sts, Rev St st on 1 st, chart on 17 sts, Rev St st on 1 st, Cable on 4 sts, Rev St st on 1 st, St st on 2 (6-9-13) sts. Work as established until 21 (23-25-27)" from beginning or desired length to shoulder. Right side facing, work across 31 (33-34-37) sts, leave on holder, work on next 27 (31-35-37) sts and leave on holder for back of neck, work on last 31 (33-34-37) sts and leave on holder.

Front: Work as for back until 14 (16-18-20)" from beg. Right side facing, work 42 (46-49-53) sts and leave remaining sts on holder. (Note: If working a man's pullover, begin with wrong side facing to reverse directions.) Turn, cast on 5 sts at beg of row for placket [47 (51-54-58) sts] and work on these 5 sts in Garter st and as established to end of row. Work even until 18¹/₂ (20¹/₂-22¹/₂-24¹/₂)" from beg. Wrong side facing, bind off 3 sts at beg of row (neck edge), work on next 9 (11-13-14) sts and leave on holder for front of neck, work to end of row. Then, dec 1 st at neck edge every right-side row 4 times. Work even on remaining 31 (33-34-37) sts until same length as back to shoulder. Leave sts on holder.

To complete other side, work across first 5 sts from holder in Garter st and as established to end of row. Work even for 1¹/₄". Right side facing, k2, yo, k2 tog for first buttonhole, work to end of row. Work 2nd buttonhole 3" higher. At 18¹/₂ (20¹/₂-22¹/₂-24¹/₂)" from beg, begin shaping neck and complete as for first side reversing shaping.

Sleeves: With smaller needles, cast on 46 (46-50-50) sts. Row 1: K 0 (0-2-2), *p2, k2, p2, Cable on 4 sts; rep from *, end p2, k2, p2, k 0 (0-2-2). Row 2: K on k, p on p. Work these 2 rows for 3", inc 9 sts evenly in last row as follows: Inc 3 sts before lst Cable, 3 sts between 1st and 3rd Cable, 3 sts to end of row—55 (55-59-59) sts. Then, with larger needles, work across as follows: St st on 8 (8-10-10) sts, Rev St st on 1 st, Cable on 4 sts, Rev St st on 1 st, Pattern st on 27 sts, Rev St st on 1 st, Cable on 4 sts, Rev St st on 1 st, St st on 8 (8-10-10) sts. Work as established, inc 1 st each end every 1 (³/₄-³/₄-³/₄)" 13 (16-17-20) times, working new sts in St st—81 (87-93-99) sts. Work even until 18 (18¹/₂-19¹/₂-20¹/₂)" from beginning or desired length to underarms. Bind off all sts.

Collar: Join shoulders using the knitted seam method. Right side facing with 16" circular needle, work across 9 (11-13-14) sts from right front holder, pick up and k 18 sts on side of neck, work across 27 (31-35-37) sts from back holder, evenly inc 1 (3-5-1) sts across [28 (34-40-38) sts], pick up and k 18 sts

and wash it with a mild detergent in hot water, then rinse well in clear hot water. Do not handle the wool too much, because that will make it felt.
SPINNING TECHNIQUE: Supported long draw.
YARN
weight: Worsted (5 stitches/inch).
yards per pound: 870.
number of plies: 3.
singles t.p.i.: 5.
plying t.p.i.: 3.

on side of neck, work across 9 (11-13-14) sts from left front holder—82 (92-102-102) sts. Wrong side facing, work across as follows: *K2, p2, Cable on 4 sts, p2; rep from *, end k2. Right side facing, k on k, p on p. Work as established for 3". Bind off all sts.

Finishing: Measure 9 (9$\frac{1}{2}$-10-10$\frac{1}{2}$)" on each side of shoulder seams and place markers on armhole edges. Set in sleeves between markers, stretching slightly to fit. Sew underarm and side seams. Slip stitch end of left placket to inside. Sew buttons opposite buttonholes.

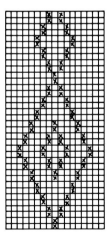

□ = Stockinette stitch background
☒ = purl on right-side rows
   knit on wrong-side rows

Maine Island sheep. Photo courtesy of Wildwood.

6 ANGORA AND SILK PULLOVER

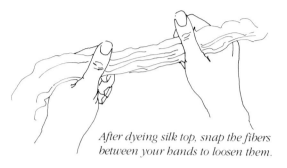

After dyeing silk top, snap the fibers between your hands to loosen them.

What to do with small amounts of truly unusual fibers? We had just 5 ounces of lovely white angora, and a very high-quality silk which we wanted to use to best advantage. We had one very fuzzy, matte fiber and one very smooth, lustrous fiber, and we wanted these fibers to retain their individuality but to be brought together harmoniously in the garment.

Past experience with a pure-angora sweater told us that although the swatch was not outrageously fuzzy the finished sweater was, and we didn't want the angora to completely dominate the silk in this new garment. As a result, we used two two-ply yarns: one of pure silk, and one of silk plied with angora. These two different yarns were perfectly matched in color tones.

Because the body of this garment would be pure silk, we knew it ran the risk of falling flat next to the angora's fluffy texture. We decided to counteract this tendency by working the body in moss stitch and by shifting the silk's color slightly. We dyed the silk before we began to spin, selecting a light shade of yellow acid dye which would warm up the silk but would not create a high contrast with the white angora.

When silk is dyed in raw form, it looks like a mashed-up mess until you begin to work with it. It's gummed up, and you need to snap it between your hands to loosen and separate the fibers before you can begin to draw it out. (When knitting, we also discovered that the silk yarn had so little stretch that it felt like string. The finished sweater, however, feels wonderful.)

The same design would be interesting if the angora were dyed in bright colors and used with natural ivory silk, if it were worked in pastels, or in black angora with navy silk, or if a single fiber were used for the entire garment and all the contrast came from the stitch textures. Some funny, subtle color changes you don't normally think of would be effective here.

The fibers made us decide on a more formal sweater, suitable for the office or evening wear, with delicate buttons and no ribbing at the neck. We had to keep in mind the limited quantities of the angora/silk yarn, so we worked from the top down, making a V-shaped yoke of angora/silk on both front and back. We could keep an eye on the

FIBER

type and source: White angora from Wildhaere Farm; combed *Bombyx mori* silk top from Fallbrook House.

characteristics: The angora is soft and lofty; fiber length is 3-4″. The silk is very fine, with a lovely sheen; fiber length is comparable to the angora.

preparation: The angora was carded lightly on hand cards with fine card clothing and spun directly from the rolag. The silk was dyed, snapped and fluffed, and then spun.

DYEING

dye type and source: Acid dye. We used Craftsman's acid dyes from The Ruggery.

process: Wind the silk into skein form, tie it very loosely in four places, wash it in warm water and detergent, then rinse and leave to soak in the final rinse water. In a stainless steel or enamel pan on the stove, mix ½ cup of white vinegar per pound of dry yarn weight with enough water to let the yarn float loosely. Wearing rubber gloves, prepare a 1% dye stock solution by mixing 1 tablespoon of dye powder in 1 pint of boiling water, using a pint jar with a good lid to store the solution. We then used 1 tablespoon of this stock solution in the dyepot; we wanted only to tint the silk. Lift the wet silk out of the water and plunge it all at once into the dyepot. Stir gently for 5

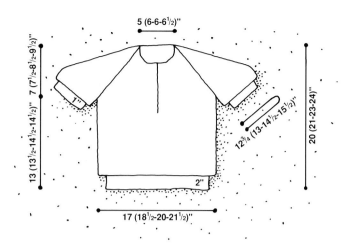

5 (6-6-6½)"

7 (7½-8½-9½)"

13 (13½-14½-14½)"

1"

12¾ (13-14½-15½)"

20 (21-23-24)"

2"

17 (18½-20-21½)"

minutes, then remove it and place it in a vinegar/water solution and heat for 30 minutes to set the dye.

SPINNING TECHNIQUE: Sliding long draw for angora, sliding short draw for silk.

YARN

weight: Light worsted (5.5 stitches/inch).

yards per pound: Angora/silk, 1150; pure silk, 1050.

number of plies: 2.

singles t.p.i.: 5-6.

plying t.p.i.: 2-3.

quantity of yarn—when we ran out, the yoke would be done. You could use any fiber which is in short supply this way, including leftovers. The sweater is waist-length, with short sleeves, and relatively lightweight; it would work well under a suit jacket. We added a little extra contrast with a different yarn at the lower edges of the front, back, and sleeves.

KNITTING INSTRUCTIONS

Instructions are for finished size 34". Changes for sizes 37", 40", and 43" are in parentheses.

Materials: Angora and silk, spun to light worsted weight. Plied angora on silk: 5½ (6-7-8) ounces or 395 (430-500-575) yards (A); plied silk on silk: 4¼ (4¾-5¾-6¼) ounces or 275 (310-375-410) yards (B). One pair each size 2 and 4 needles or size to obtain correct gauge. One size E crochet hook. Seven ⅜" buttons, 8 markers.

Gauge: In St st with size 4 needles, 5.5 sts and 7.5 rows = 1".

Stitches Used: *Stockinette stitch. Seed stitch—Rows 1 & 2:* K1, p1. *Rows 3 & 4:* P1, k1. Repeat rows 1-4 for pattern.

Note: Pullover is worked from the neck down.

Body: With larger needles and A, cast on 40 (46-46-48) sts. Work as follows: Row 1: K1, place marker, k1, place marker, k3, place marker, k1, place marker, k 27 (33-33-35) sts, place marker, k1, place marker, k3, place marker, k1, place marker, k2—markers indicate raglan "seams." Row 2 and all wrong-side rows: Purl. Row 3: Knit across row, inc by knitting in front and back of st before first raglan seam marker and in st after second raglan seam marker; repeat for each raglan seam—8 increases. Repeat this increase row every right-side row 27 (28-32-35) times total. At the same time, at 1" from beg, inc at each end of needle by knitting in front and back of first st and in st before last st every right-side row 6 times. Then, cast on 6 (9-9-10) sts at beg of next 2 rows. Continue working raglan increases as before until you have 280 (300-332-360) sts on needle. Separate and place sts on holders as follows: First 41 (45-49-53) sts for half of front, 58 (60-68-74) sts for first sleeve, 82 (90-98-106) sts for back, 58 (60-68-74) sts for second sleeve, 41 (45-49-53) sts for half of front.

Sleeves: Place sts from one sleeve holder back onto larger needle. Working in St st, cast on 6 sts at beg of next 2 rows, then work even on obtained 70 (72-80-86) sts until 2 (2-2^1/$_2$-3)" from beg, evenly dec 13 (11-17-19) sts across last row—57 (61-63-67) sts. With smaller needles, right side facing, and B, work as follows: Row 1: K1, *p1, k1. Row 2: P1, *k1, p1. Repeat these 2 rows for 1". With larger needles and A, work 2 more rows. Bind off all sts in rib.

Back: Place sts from back holder onto larger needle. With A, working in St st, cast on 6 sts at beg of next 2 rows—94 (102-110-118) sts. Then, work pattern as follows: Rows 1 & 2: With B, work in Moss st on first and last 2 sts, and with A, work St st on center sts. Rows 3 & 4: As for rows 1 & 2 but work Moss st on 4 sts at beg and end of row. Continue in this manner working 2 more sts in Moss st on each side of piece every right-side row until all sts are worked in Moss st. Continue with B only until 11 (11^1/$_2$-12-12^1/$_2$)" from armholes, evenly dec 11 sts across last row—83 (91-99-107) sts. With smaller needles and A, work in rib as for sleeves for 16 rows. With larger needles and B, work 2 more rows. Bind off all sts in rib.

Front: Place sts from right front holder back onto larger needle. With right side facing and A, working in St st, cast on 6 sts at beg of first row—47 (51-55-59) sts. Purl back. Then, begin working pattern as for back on armhole edges only, until 18 sts are worked in Moss st ending with a right-side row. Leave sts on holder. Repeat procedure for sts on left front holder. To join front and back, with wrong side facing, work across sts on needle, then across sts from right front holder—94 (102-110-118) sts. Complete front as for back.

Neck Edge: With crochet hook and B, attach yarn at corner of left front. Work in single crochet down left side of front opening, then up right side of front opening evenly spacing seven "chain-2" buttonloops, positioning the top loop at upper edge of neck. Then, continue around neck opening keeping stitch tension fairly firm. Sc to first st at corner. For second row, work in sc on neck edge only, but work from left to right instead. Fasten off.

Finishing: Sew underarm and side seams. Sew buttons opposite buttonholes.

Luxury fibers sometimes come in small handfuls, yet ask to become very special garments; with attention to detail, they can.

58

7 ANGORA EYELET PULLOVER

Ah, the pleasures and challenges of pure angora! As we mentioned in the discussion of the preceding sweater, an angora swatch is not as fuzzy as the finished sweater. Keep this in mind. Whatever you do with angora, its dominant impression will come from the soft halo of fibers that rises from the surface. Thinking of spinning a textured yarn? There's no point. It won't show. Planning a complex combination of stitches? You'll waste the time counting rows.

We did decide to work a subtle clover eyelet stitch in this sweater, because it plays with the light and the minor natural variations in the black angora and breaks up the monotony. It doesn't show much—but we think it was worth the minor effort to use it.

The natural black angora we worked with had a lot of color variation, both between handfuls of fiber and within individual fibers: the tips were black and the inner ends were light gray. We decided to leave it undyed.

Obviously, this would be a sweater to dress up in, not one to wear to the woodpile. Since angora is eight times warmer than wool, a short, V-neck sweater with short set-in sleeves seemed like a wise choice. Instead of leaving the V-neck plain, we placed one small, jewel-like button at the tip of the V.

Since the rabbits keep themselves very clean, angora does not need to be washed or scoured. Stay away from drafts or breezes when carding or spinning it. You'll find you can control the fiber better with hand cards (fine card clothing, like that on cards made for cotton, helps), but it is possible to work with a drum carder. Our carder worked better on later batts than it did on the first ones; persevere! For spinning, Rachael arranged the rolags on a big tray, then laid them along her arm to support them while she was spinning.

FIBER
type and source: Natural black angora from Wildhaere Farm.
characteristics: Soft and lofty; fiber length is 3-4″.
preparation: Batches were hand-mixed, to avoid light and dark areas, then lightly carded on fine cards and spun directly from rolags.
SPINNING TECHNIQUE: Sliding long draw.
YARN
weight: Sport (5.5 stitches/inch in pattern stitch).
yards per pound: 1300.
number of plies: 2.
singles t.p.i.: 8.
plying t.p.i.: 4-5.

Natural black angora requires delicate handling—in the carding, spinning, and designing—but how many fancy sweaters are really warm and comfortable?

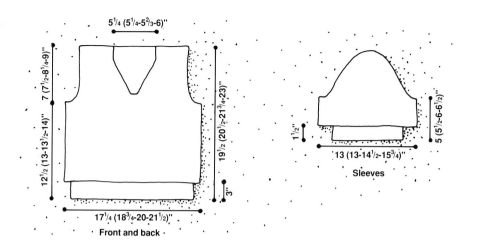

5¼ (5¼-5⅔-6)"

7 (7½-8¼-9)"

12½ (13-13½-14)"

19½ (20½-21¾-23)"

3"

17¼ (18¾-20-21½)"

Front and back

1½"

13 (13-14½-15¾)"

Sleeves

5 (5½-6-6½)"

KNITTING INSTRUCTIONS

Instructions are for finished size 34½". Changes for sizes 37½", 40", and 43" are in parentheses.

Materials: Wildehaere Farm's angora, spun to sport weight: 7 (8-9¼-10½) ounces or 570 (650-755-855) yards. One pair each size 3 and 5 needles or size to obtain correct gauge. One 24" size 3 circular needle. One ⅜" button.

Gauge: In Pattern stitch with size 5 needles, 5.5 sts and 8 rows = 1".

Stitched Used: *Pattern stitch—Rows 1 & 3:* Knit. *Rows 2 and all wrong side rows:* Purl. *Row 5:* K2, yo, sl 1, k2 tog, psso, yo, *k5, yo, sl 1, k2 tog, psso, yo; rep from *, end k2. *Row 7:* K3, yo, ssk, *k6, yo, ssk; rep from *, end k2. *Rows 9 & 11:* Knit. *Row 13:* K1, *k5, yo, sl 1, k2 tog, psso, yo; rep from *, end k6. *Row 15:* K7, *yo, ssk, k6; rep from *. *Row 16:* As row 2. Repeat these 16 rows for pattern.

Back: With smaller needles, cast on 88 (96-104-112) sts. Work in k1, p1 rib for 3", inc 7 sts evenly in last row—95 (103-111-119) sts. Then, with larger needles, work in Pattern stitch. AT THE SAME TIME, at 12½ (13-13½-14)" from beginning, shape armhole: Bind off 5 sts at beginning of next 2 rows, then dec 1 st each end every other row 6 times. Work even on remaining 73 (81-89-97) sts until 6 (6½-7¼-8)" above armhole. Work across 26 (30-33-36) sts and leave remaining sts on holder. Then, working on this side only, bind off 2 sts at neck edge 2 times. Work even on remaining 22 (26-29-32) sts until 7 (7½-8¼-9)" above armhole. Shape shoulders: Bind off 5 (6-7-8) sts at beginning of next 3 right-side rows, then bind off remaining 7 (8-8-8) sts.

To complete other side, leave center 21 (21-23-25) sts on holder for back of neck, and shape neck and shoulder as for first side reversing shapings.

Front: Work as for back until 12½ (13-13½-14)" from beginning. Begin armhole shaping and neck shaping as follows: Right side facing, bind off 5 sts, work on 40 (44-48-52) sts and leave remaining sts on holder. Working on this side only, continue armhole shaping as for back and work even on neck edge until 34 (38-42-46) sts remain. Then, work neck edge as follows: Dec 1 st at end of next right-side row, then again every ⅓" 12 (12-13-14) times. Work even on remaining 22 (26-29-32) sts until 7 (7½-8¼-9)" above armhole. Shape shoulder as for back.

Angora takes acid dyes well. Again, cool colors such as blue and violet combine very pleasingly with the natural color. You might try dyeing the raw fiber (use small onion bags to contain it in the dyebath) or the finished yarn.

To complete other side, place sts from front holder onto needle and bind off center 5 sts, then work in same manner as for first side, reversing armhole and neck shaping.

Sleeves: With smaller needles, cast on 50 (52-54-56) sts. Work in k1, p1 rib for $1^1/_2$", inc 21 (19-25-31) sts evenly in last row—71 (71-79-97) sts. Then, with larger needles, beg working Pattern stitch and AT THE SAME TIME, at 5 ($5^1/_2$-6-$6^1/_2$)" from beginning, shape armhole and cap: Bind off 5 sts at beg of next 2 rows, then dec 1 st each end every 4 rows 3 times, then every other row until 19 sts remain. Bind off 3 sts at beg of next 4 rows, then bind off remaining 7 sts.

Neckband: Sew shoulder seams. With right-side facing and circular needle, beginning at right edge of front placket opening, pick up and k 7 sts to point where V shaping begins, pick up and k 2 sts at corner, pick up and k 36 (40-44-48) sts on right side of front neck to shoulder seam, pick up and k 7 sts on back neck edge, work across 21 (21-23-25) sts from back neck holder, pick up and k 7 sts on back neck edge to shoulder seam, pick up and k 36 (40-44-48) sts on left side of front neck to point where placket begins, pick up and k 2 sts at corner, then pick up and k 7 sts on left edge of placket opening. Work back and forth on these 125 (133-143-153) sts in k1, p1 rib for $^1/_2$". Next right-side row, keeping in rib pattern, work 4 sts, k2 tog, yo (one buttonhole made), work to end of row. Work even in rib until band is 1" wide. Bind off all sts in rib.

Finishing: Sew edge of placket at center front lapping right edge over left. Set in sleeves at armhole opening. Sew underarm and side seams. Sew button opposite buttonhole.

8 BOHUS CARDIGAN

For this sweater, we started with the yarn. Our wool from the Shetland Isles came in lovely natural colors—a wide variety of values in browns, moorits (red-browns), grays, and white—and we wanted to use them together. A cardigan with a patterned yoke seemed like a good possibility, and we looked to the traditional Bohus sweaters of Sweden for inspiration. Depending on the colors you choose, this sweater would work well for men or women so we have it multi-sized.

Shetland fleeces normally yield between 2 and 3 pounds of wool after skirting. A few may provide up to 5 pounds, and we selected a larger fleece for the main color of our sweater. It was, conveniently, a medium-value color.

The traditional Bohus sweaters originated in a specific Swedish workshop in the late 1930s. Characteristics of the style include a combination of bright colors of fine wool yarn (sometimes blended with angora), small color patterns worked with two colors per row, small texture patterns (a combination of knit and purl stitches on the right side of the garment), and a circular yoke.

We wanted to make our sweater more "American" by using the naturals and subtle accents. We chose to use angora, but as a separate yarn and not a component of a wool blend, thinking that the contrast in texture and color of the angora would go well with the relief effect obtained by the pattern's purled stitches. Our sweater is also worked with larger yarn than the originals, at a gauge of 5 stitches/inch. This makes both spinning and knitting go faster.

Our final color choices included four of the natural Shetland colors, two natural angoras, and one dyed (light blue) angora. We could have used many dyed colors, instead of the naturals. The sweater would be very pretty in soft grays, perhaps with a red accent. Because only small amounts of the accent colors are required, a yoke like this is an excellent place to use leftovers. Be sure, though, that your yarns are all of the same weight so your gauge is consistent.

Rachael declared the spinning of this yarn "glorious." The fleece contains both short, soft, undercoat fibers and longer fibers; the yarn lofted nicely and blossomed more when it was washed. For this reason, extra sampling is necessary; it's easy to get too big a yarn!

FIBER

type and source: Shetland Island wool from Wildwood; angora.

characteristics: The wool is a fine grade, with close-set crimp; it came in raw form, and was quite free of any vegetation. Fiber length is 3-6″.

preparation: The wool was picked, scoured, teased, and then drum carded. The batts were pulled to a manageable size for spinning.

SPINNING TECHNIQUE: Sliding long draw for both fibers.

DYEING

dye type and source: Acid dyes. We used Craftsman's dyes from The Ruggery.

process: A 1-ounce skein of white angora was dyed light blue by adding one drop of a 1% stock solution of blue dye

(continued)

Bohus sweaters originated in Sweden and feature round yokes, patterned with both color and texture. In ours, several colors of natural Shetland wool are accented with small amounts of other colors and fibers.

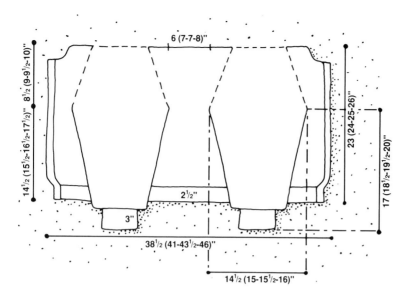

KNITTING INSTRUCTIONS

Instructions are for finished size 37½". Changes for sizes 40", 42½", and 45" are in parentheses.

Materials: Wildwood's Shetland Isle wool, spun to worsted weight: 2¼ (3-3¾-4¼) ounces or 120 (160-200-230) yards gray (A), 12½ (14¼-16-17¼) ounces or 670 (765-860-925) yards light moorit (B), 2 (2¾-3½-4¼) ounces or 105 (145-165-225) yards dark moorit (C), 1 (1½-2-2½) ounces or 50 (80-105-135) yards black (D). Angora: ¾ ounce or 40 yards each white (E), fawn (F), and blue (G). One each 29" size 5 and 7 circular needles, or size to obtain correct gauge. Eight (8-8-9) ⅝" buttons.

Gauge: In St st with size 7 needle, 5 sts = 1". In Color pattern, with size 7 needle, 6.5 rows = 1".

Note: Body is worked in one piece.

Stitches Used: *Stockinette stitch. Seed stitch—Row 1:* *K1, p1. *Row 2 and all subsequent rows:* P the k sts and k the p sts as they face you. *Color pattern—Row 1 (right side):* With E, purl. *Row 2:* P1 D, *p1 E, p1 D. *Row 3:* K1 D, *k1 B, k1 D. *Row 4:* P1 D, *p1 B, p1 D. *Row 5:* With A, knit. *Row 6:* K3 A, *p1 C, k3 A. *Row 7:* K1 C, *k1 A, k3 C; rep from *, end k1 A, k1 C. *Row 8:* With C, knit. *Row 9:* With B, knit. *Row 10:* P1 B, *p1 A, p3 B; rep from *, end p1 A, p1 B. *Row 11:* K3 G, *k1 A, k3 G; rep from *. *Row 12:* K3 G, *p1 A, k3 G; rep from *. *Row 13:* K1 C, *k1 A, k1 C. *Row 14:* K3 C, *p1 A, k3 C. *Row 15:* With A, knit. *Row 16:* P3 A, *p1 D, p3 A; rep from *. *Row 17:* K1 D, *k1 A, k3 D; rep from *, end k1 A, k1 D. *Row 18:* With D, purl. *Row 19:* P1 F, *k1 B, p1 F. *Row 20:* P1 F, *p1 B, p1 F. *Row 21:* With B, purl. *Row 22:* P3 A, *p1 B, p3 A. *Row 23:* K2 A, *k2 B, k2 A; rep from *, end k1 B. *Row 24:* P2 B, *p1 A, p3 B; rep from *, end p1 A. *Row 25:* P3 C, *k1 A, p3 C. *Row 26:* With A, purl.

Body: With smaller needles and B, cast on 177 (189-201-213) sts. Work across as follows: Row 1: Seed st on 5 sts, k1, *p1, k1; rep from * to last 5 sts, Seed st on 5 sts. Row 2: Seed st on 5 sts p1, *k1, p1; rep from * to last 5 sts, Seed st on 5 sts. Work as established for ½". On next right-side row, in left band for women, right for men, work first buttonhole as follows: K1, p2 tog, yo, p1, k1, work to end of row as established. Work even until 2½" from beg, inc 16 sts evenly in last row (do not make inc in buttonhole band)—193 (205-217-229) sts. Leave first and last 5 sts on holders. Then, with larger need-

to the dyepot. Follow the process we described for sweater 2, Novelty Yarn Pullover.

YARN
weight: Worsted (5 stitches/inch).
yards per pound: 860.
number of plies: 2.
singles t.p.i.: 5-6.
plying t.p.i.: 3.

les, work rows 1 to 14 of Color pattern on remaining 183 (195-207-219) sts. Then work even with B only in St st until 14$^1/_2$ (15-15$^1/_2$-16)" from beg. Divide for underarm and place sts on holders as follows: Work on 40 (43-46-49) sts, bind off 10 sts, work on 83 (89-95-101) sts, bind off 10 sts, work on 40 (43-46-49) sts. Leave stitches on holder.

Sleeves: With smaller needles and B, cast on 45 (47-49-51) sts. Work as follows: Row 1: K1, *p1, k1. Row 2: P1, *k1, p1. Work even for 3", inc 14 (16-18-20) sts evenly in last row—59 (63-67-71) sts. With larger needles, work rows 1 to 14 of Color pattern. Then with B only work in St st, inc 1 st each end of 1st row then every 1$^3/_4$ (2-2-2)" 6 (6-7-7) times more. Work even on obtained 73 (77-83-87) sts until 17 (18$^1/_2$-19$^1/_2$-20)" from beg. Bind off 5 sts at beg and end of next row. Leave remaining 63 (67-73-77) sts on holder.

Yoke: With right side facing, larger needle, and B, work across in St st as follows: On 40 (43-46-49) sts from right front holder, work across 63 (67-73-77) sts from first sleeve holder, work across 83 (89-95-101) sts from back holder, work across 63 (67-73-77) sts from second sleeve holder, work across 40 (43-46-49) sts from left front holder. Work back, evenly dec 2 sts across—287 (307-331-351) sts. Continue rest of yoke following Color pattern working shaping as follows: Size 37$^1/_2$: Evenly dec 36 sts across on rows 5, 15, 31, 35, and 41, and evenly dec 24 sts across rows 47 and 52; about 8$^1/_2$" above armhole. Size 40: Evenly dec 40 sts on rows 5, 15, 34, 47, 53, and 60; about 9" above armhole. Size 42$^1/_2$: Evenly dec 44 sts on rows 5, 15, 34, 52, 57, and 61; about 9$^1/_2$" above armhole. Size 45: Evenly dec 44 sts on rows 5, 15, 35, and 52, and evenly dec 52 sts across row 57 and 48 sts across row 67; about 10" above armhole. AT THE SAME TIME, at 6$^1/_2$ (7-7$^1/_2$-8)" above armhole, leave first 10 (12-12-14) sts on holder at beg of next 2 rows, then dec 1 st each end every right-side row 4 times. When all yoke and neck shapings are completed, leave remaining 31 (35-35-39) sts on holder for back of neck.

Buttonhole Band: With smaller needle, pick up 5 sts from left buttonhole band holder (right for men) and work in Seed st with B until band is long enough, slightly stretched, to fit on side of front to neck edge. Leave sts on holder. Work other side in same manner, evenly spacing 6 (6-6-7) buttonholes in center of band and planning to have one more in center of neck band.

Neckband: With smaller needle and B, work in Seed st on 5 sts from right band holder, k across 10 (12-12-14) sts from right front holder, pick up and k 13 sts on right side of neck, work across 31 (35-35-39) sts from back holder, pick up and k 13 sts on left side of neck, work across 10 (12-12-14) sts from left front holder, work in Seed st on 5 sts from left band holder. Work back and forth on these 87 (95-95-103) sts as for lower body rib for $1/2$", work last buttonhole, work for $1/2$" more. Bind off all sts.

Finishing: Sew underarm and sleeve seams. Sew buttonhole bands to front edges. Sew buttons opposite buttonholes.

FIBER

type and source: Corriedale top from R. H. Lindsay; mohair from Gerald Whitaker; Italian silk from Fallbrook House; cinnamon silk, tussah silk, and camel from Straw Into Gold; white angora from Wildhaere Farm.

characteristics: The fibers for this sweater varied a great deal, from the comparatively coarse mohair to the superfine silk and angora.

preparation: All fibers were ready to use in commercial top form or were, in the case of the angora, clean and spinnable.

SPINNING TECHNIQUE: Supported long draw.

YARN

weight: Bulky (worked at 4 stitches/inch).

yards per pound: Corriedale, 640; other fibers, 960.

number of plies: 2.

singles t.p.i.: 4-5.

plying t.p.i.: 2-3.

FIBER COMBINATIONS (plied with Corriedale):
    Corriedale (both plies) (MC)
    white angora (A)
    tussah silk (B)
    cinnamon silk (C)
    camel (D)
    blend of camel and
        Corriedale (F)
    white Italian silk (G)
    mohair (H)
two-ply silk:
    tussah silk and Italian silk (E)

This patchwork-type design is a good way to use small amounts of luxury fibers. We were dealing with the contrasts between the various natural colorations and the textures of the fibers, wanting to keep the emphasis on those elements. Although we talked about using some texture in the yarns, we decided to keep their structure and the sweater's basic shape simple.

One of the problems in using a variety of fibers in the same garment is having yarns that are compatible, so certain areas aren't stiff or sagging. We solved this by using one ply of Corriedale in all but one of the yarns (a 2-ply silk).

To keep chart-reading easy, we worked the same set of patterns on both front and back of the sweater. A short, ribbed yoke at the shoulder, a dropped shoulder, and a softly rounded neck opening framed the pattern without offering competition.

You could work this sweater in brighter colors, or use other stitches. Be sure to sample, though, because keeping the gauge consistent is the key to this sweater's success.

KNITTING INSTRUCTIONS

Instructions are for finished size 38". Changes for sizes 40", 42", and 44" are in parentheses.

Materials: Yarn spun to bulky weight. Corriedale top: $10^1/_2$ ($11^1/_4$-$12^1/_2$-$13^1/_4$) ounces or 420 (450-505-530) yards (MC); Corriedale plied with *white angora* 55 yards (A); Corriedale plied with *tussah silk* 90 yards (B); Corriedale plied with *cinnamon silk* 50 yards (C); Corriedale plied with *camel* 40 yards (D); *tussah silk* plied with *Italian silk* 40 yards (E); Corriedale plied with a blend of *camel and Corriedale* 45 yards (F); Corriedale plied with *white Italian silk, spun thick-and-thin* 55 yards (G); Corriedale plied with *mohair* 115 yards (H). One pair each size 6 and 8 needles or size to obtain correct gauge. One cable needle (cn).

Gauge: In St st with size 8 needles and MC, 4 sts=1".

Stitches Used: *Stockinette stitch. Garter stitch. Reverse Stockinette stitch. Seed stitch—Row 1:* K1, p1. *Row 2 and all subsequent rows:* P the k sts and k the p sts as they face you. *Moss stitch—Row 1:* K1, p1. *Rows 2 & 4:* K on k, p on p. *Row 3:* P1, k1. Repeat these 4 rows for pattern. *Eyelet stitch—Row 1:* K. *Row 2:* P. *Row 3:* K1, *yo, k2 tog. *Row 4:* P. *Rows 5 & 6:* As rows 1 & 2. Repeat these 6 rows for pattern. *Berry stitch—Row 1:* P1, k3. *Row 2:* In one stitch work (k1, yo, k1), p3 tog. *Row 3:* K3, p1. *Row 4:* P3 tog, in one stitch work (k1, yo, k1). Repeat these 4 rows for pattern. *Big cable—Row 1:* P3, *k6, p3; rep from *, end p1. *Rows 2, 4, & 6:* K on k, p on p. *Row 3:* P3, *sl 3 to cn, hold in back, k3, k3 from cn, p3; rep from *, end p1. *Row 5:* As row 1. Repeat these 6 rows for pattern. *Small cable—Row 1:* P3, *k2, p4. *Rows 2 & 4:* *K4, p2; rep from *, end k3. *Row 3:* P3, *k next 2 sts tog, leave on needle and k first st again, drop both sts off needle together, p4. Repeat these 4 rows for pattern. *Ridge stitch—Rows 1 & 4:* K. *Rows 2 & 3:* P.

Back: With smaller needles and MC, cast on 69 (73-77-81) sts. Row 1: K1, *p1, k1. Row 2: P1, *k1, p1. Work in rib for $1^{1}/_{2}$", inc 8 sts evenly in last row— 77 (81-85-89) sts. Then, with larger needles, work with MC in St st for 4 (5-6-7)", then begin working chart placing pattern stitches and appropriate yarn in designated areas. Once chart is complete, work in rib as for lower edge for $1^{1}/_{2}$" back measures approximately 22 (23-24-25)" from beg. Next row, work 21 (22-24-25) sts and leave on holder, bind off next 35 (37-37-39) sts for back of neck, work remaining sts and leave on holder.

Front: Work as for back until 1" before shoulder. Next row, work on 27 (28-30-31) sts and leave remaining sts on holder. Working on this side only, bind off 3 sts at neck edge every other row 2 times. Work even on remaining 21 (22-24-25) sts until same length as back to shoulder. Leave sts on holder. To complete other side, bind off center 23 (25-25-27) sts and work on remaining sts as for first side, reversing shaping.

Sleeves: Join shoulders using the knitted seam method. Then, measure $9^{3}/_{4}$ (10-$10^{1}/_{4}$-$10^{1}/_{2}$)" on each side of shoulder seams and place markers on armhole edge. Then, with larger needles and B, pick up and k 79 (81-83-85) sts between markers. Work pattern on sleeves as follows: With B, work 3 rows Garter st; with A, 6 rows St st; with F, 4 rows Seed st; with H, 6 rows Eyelet st; with C, 6 rows St st; with G, 4 rows Ridge st; with D, 4 rows Moss st; (work 2 rows St st with MC, then k2 rows with E) 2 times; with MC, work 9 rows St st and, wrong side facing, k 10th row. Repeat these last 10 rows to cuff. AT THE SAME TIME, dec 1 st each end every 1" 13 (14-14-15) times.

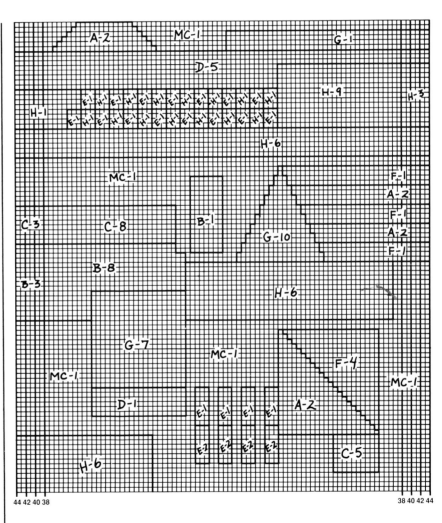

44 42 40 38   38 40 42 44

1—Stockinette	MC
2—Garter	A—Corriedale/white angora
3—Reverse stockinette	B—Corriedale/tussah silk
4—Seed	C—Corriedale/cinnamon silk
5—Moss	D—Corriedale/camel
6—Eyelet	E—tussah silk/Italian silk
7—Berry	F—Corriedale/camel-Corriedale
8—Big cable	G—thick-thin Corriedale/Italian silk
9—Small cable	H—Corriedale/mohair
10—Ridge	

Work even on remaining 53 (53-55-55) sts until 14½ (15-15½-16)" from beg, dec 20 (18-20-18) sts evenly in last row—33 (35-35-37) sts. With smaller needles and B, work in rib as for lower back for 2½", then work with A for ½" more. Bind off all sts in rib.

Finishing: Sew underarm and side seams.

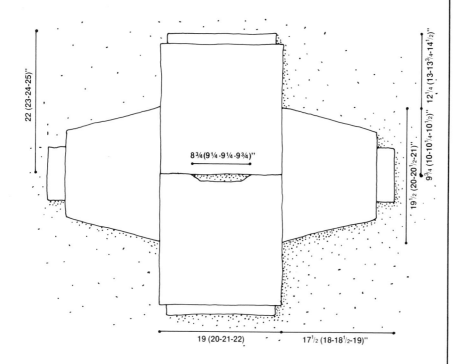

22 (23-24-25)"

8¾(9¼-9¼-9¾)"

9¾ (10-10¼-10½)"

12¼ (13-13¾-14½)"

19½ (20-20½-21)"

19 (20-21-22)   17½ (18-18½-19)"

FIBER

type and source: Camel down and *Bombyx mori* silk from Straw Into Gold.

characteristics: The camel down is soft, fine, and short; it comes in small batts, ready to spin. The silk is a combed top in brick form, with a fiber length of 3″.

preparation: The camel down was split into small handfuls and pulled to a manageable size for spinning. The silk was dyed, fluffed, pulled, and spun.

DYEING

dye type and source: Acid dye. We used Craftsman's dye from The Ruggery.

process: The silk was wound into a skein, tied loosely in four places, washed in warm water and detergent, then rinsed and left to soak. Dye powder weighing 3% of the dry weight of the silk was wet and then added to

(continued)

Right: Although the spinning and color pattern in this vest look sophisticated, both are quite simple—and very rewarding (this page).

Left: "Leftovers" are a goldmine, as you can see in this Fair Isle vest.

This is an ideal project for less experienced color knitters, since a slip-stitch pattern gives the illusion of color stranding without the extra work.

Two fibers of opposing qualities were chosen for this sweater—the camel is matte, the silk very shiny. We reinforced this idea by dyeing the silk and leaving the camel natural. There were three possible 2-ply combinations of these fibers—camel on camel, camel on silk, and silk on silk. We used each yarn for its particular strength: the pure camel was used for all ribbings, since it was the most elastic; the second combination became the background color; and the third yarn (pure silk) was used for the slip-stitch pattern.

The plying and the slip-stitch pattern also allowed us to tone down the high contrast within the body of the sweater. We were able to produce a vertical line in the main body sections, wrapping our yarn twice to extend the slip stitches over several rows. Because of the pattern stitch, we used a smoothly spun yarn.

This versatile design has a scoop neck and a small placket opening. The camel would be too warm for summer wear, but if made with cooler fibers the sweater could be worn as a summer top. We'd like to see the same natural-colored camel knitted up with a mulberry-colored silk. Any color combination, stitch, or fiber could be substituted if the gauge matches. It would be fun to use something like angora or a yarn which has been heavily textured in the spinning process instead of the silk.

KNITTING INSTRUCTIONS

Instructions are for finished size 34". Changes for sizes 36", 38", 40", and 42" are in parentheses.

Materials: Straw Into Gold's camel and silk, spun to sport weight. 2 (2$\frac{1}{4}$-2$\frac{1}{2}$-2$\frac{3}{4}$-3) ounces or 125 (140-155-170-190) yards camel (A), 2 (2$\frac{1}{4}$-2$\frac{1}{2}$-2$\frac{3}{4}$-3) ounces or 185 (210-235-260-280) yards silk (B), 3$\frac{1}{4}$ (3$\frac{1}{2}$-4-4$\frac{1}{4}$-4$\frac{3}{4}$) ounces or 255 (270-310-330-370) yards camel and silk (C). One pair each size 3 and 5 needles or size to obtain correct gauge. One 24" size 3 circular needle. Two $\frac{1}{2}$" buttons.

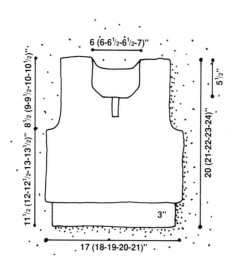

6 (6-6½-6½-7)"

5½"

8½ (9-9½-10-10½)"

11½ (12-12½-13-13½)"

20 (21-22-23-24)"

3"

17 (18-19-20-21)"

Gauge: In Pattern st with size 5 needles, 6 sts=1".

Stitches Used: *Garter stitch. Pattern stitch—Row 1:* With B, knit. *Row 2:* With B, p3, *p1 wrapping yarn around needle 2 times, p3. *Rows 3 & 5:* With C, k3, *sl 1 with yarn in back, k3. *Rows 4 & 6:* With C, p3, *sl 1 with yarn in front, p3. Repeat these 6 rows for pattern.

Note: When stopping at neck or at shoulder, if ending with row 2 of Pattern stitch, omit the double wrap across row.

Back: With smaller needles and A, cast on 95 (99-107-111-119) sts. Row 1: K1, *p1, k1. Row 2: P1, *k1, p1. Repeat these 2 rows for 3½", inc 8 sts evenly across last row—103 (107-115-119-127) sts. Then, with larger needles, work in Pattern st and AT THE SAME TIME, at 11½ (12-12½-13-13½)" from beginning, shape armhole: Bind off 6 sts at beg of next 2 rows, then dec 1 st each end every other row 6 times. Work even on remaining 79 (83-91-95-103) sts until 7 (7½-8-8½-9)" above armhole. Right side facing, work on 26 (28-30-32-34) sts, leave remaining sts on holder. Working on this side only, dec 1 st at neck edge every other row 4 times. Work even on remaining 22 (24-26-28-30) sts until 8½ (9-9½-10-10½)" above armhole. Leave sts on holder.

To complete other side, leave center 27 (27-31-31-35) sts on holder for back of neck, and work on remaining sts as for first side.

Front: Work as for back until ½ (1-1½-2-2½)" above armhole bind-off row. Work placket as follows: Work to center 5 sts, turn leaving remaining sts on holder. With A, cast on 5 sts at beg of row, k across these 5 sts, and work as established to end of row. Work on this side only keeping the 5 sts for placket in Garter st with A. Work even for 2½" on remaining 42 (44-48-50-54) sts (after armhole shaping is complete). Shape neck: At neck edge, leave 12 (12-14-14-16) sts on holder. Then, at same edge, dec 1 st every other row 8 times. Work even on remaining 22 (24-26-28-30) sts until same length as back to shoulder. Leave sts on holder.

To complete other side, work on first 5 sts from holder with A in Garter st and on remaining sts as established. Work even for 1". Right side facing, k2, yo, k2 tog for buttonhole. Continue working as established completing this side as for first side.

the dyepot, along with ½ cup of white vinegar. The silk was entered and then the dyebath was heated to 160° F. The silk was allowed to sit in the hot dyebath for 30 minutes while being stirred occasionally, then rinsed and hung to dry. (See silk notes on page 56.)
SPINNING TECHNIQUE: Supported long draw for the camel; sliding short draw for the silk.
YARN
weight: Sport (6 stitches/inch).
yards per pound: In singles, camel, 2000; silk 3000. One yarn is camel plied with itself; another is camel plied with silk; the third is silk plied with silk.
number of plies: 2.
singles t.p.i.: 6-8.
plying t.p.i.: 3-4.

Neckband: Join shoulder seams using the knitted seam method. With circular needle, right side facing, and with A, work across 12 (12-14-14-16) sts from right front holder, pick up and k 48 sts on side of neck, work across 27 (27-31-31-35) sts from back holder, pick up and k 48 sts on side of neck, work across 12 (12-14-14-16) sts from front holder. Work back and forth on these 147 (147-155-155-163) sts, working in ribbing as for lower back and keeping first and last 5 sts in Garter st. At $1/2$" from beg, right side facing, work second buttonhole, then work even until band is 1" wide. Bind off all sts in rib.

Armhole Bands: Sew side seams. With circular needle and A, begin at underarm seam and pick up and k 118 (124-130-136-142) sts around armhole opening. Work around in k1, p1 rib for 1". Bind off all sts in rib.

Finishing: Sew buttons opposite buttonholes.

11 FAIR ISLE VEST

This "leftovers" creation became one of our favorites. It happened about halfway through the series of sweaters, because our collection of extra yarn had become significant. Small quantities of Maine island fleece, angora, and Shetland wool—compatible in color and weight— suggested a Fair Isle design. A classic all-over color pattern is always a good choice for using up small quantities of yarn. The buttoned- down, scoop-neck vest can be made in a wide range of sizes, suitable for men and women. Since the natural black angora was very close in value to the silver Shetland, we dyed the angora jet black. This gave us both a contrasting color for accent and the textural contrast we wanted. We did spin the main color which pulled everything together, using 8 ounces of Merino top.

Once the color pattern was established, the vest stood its own ground with distinction. And it was completed very quickly. (You don't have to wait for leftovers to make it!) The key to success is using yarns of the same weight throughout. Fairly smooth yarns will keep the focus on the color pattern where it belongs. For a different

FIBER

type and source: Merino top from R. H. Lindsay (background), Maine island fleece and Shetland fleece from Wildwood (left over from sweaters 5 and 8), natural black angora from Wildhaere Farm (left over from sweater 7).

characteristics: Each of these fibers can be spun to produce a lightweight, soft yarn. The Merino is softest and springiest. The Maine island and Shetland wools are longer fibers, still very soft. The angora gives a different surface texture.

preparation: The Merino top was ready to pull and spin. The

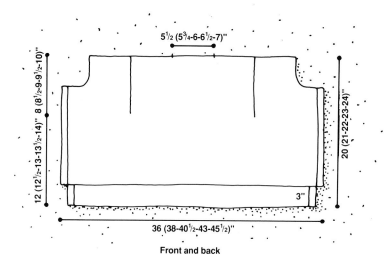

5½ (5¾-6-6½-7)"

8 (8½-9-9½-10)"

12 (12½-13-13½-14)"

20 (21-22-23-24)"

3"

36 (38-40½-43-45½)"

Front and back

look, you could change colors more frequently throughout the pattern repeat.

KNITTING INSTRUCTIONS

Instructions are for finished size 35". Changes for sizes 37", 39½", 42", 44½" are in parentheses.

Materials: Yarns spun to worsted weight. 5½ (5¾-6½-7½-8) ounces or 410 (430-485-560-600) yards Merino wool natural (A), 1¾ (1¾-2-2¼-2½) ounces or 95 (95-110-120-135) yards Shetland wool natural light gray (B), 2¼ (2½-2¾-3-3¼) ounces or 120 (135-150-165-175) yards Island fleece wool red (C), about one ounce or up to 75 yards all sizes angora black (dyed) (D). One 16" size 6 circular needle, and one each 24" size 6 and 8 circular needles or size to obtain correct gauge. Six (6-6-7-7) ½" buttons.

Gauge: In Color pattern in St st with size 8 needle, 5 sts = 1".

Stitches Used: *Stockinette stitch. Garter stitch.*

Note: Vest is worked in one piece to armhole, then fronts and back are worked separately to shoulders. Buttonhole band is worked at the same time with a separate skein of yarn.

Body: With smaller 24" needle and A, cast on 169 (181-193-205-217) sts. Work as follows: *Row 1:* K5, (p1, k1) to last 6 sts, p1, k5. *Row 2:* K6, (p1, k1) to last 5 sts, k5. Repeat these 2 rows for ribbing for ½ (¾-½-¾-½)". Right side facing, work first buttonhole as follows: K2, yo, k2 tog, work to end of row. Work even as established until 3" from beg, inc 10 sts evenly in last row—179 (191-203-215-227) sts. Do not make increases in first or last 5 sts. Then, with larger needle, work across as follows: In Garter st with A on first and last 5 sts for bands, and in St st on center 169 (181-193-205-217) sts following color chart to shoulders. AT THE SAME TIME, work 4 (4-4-5-5) more buttonholes spaced 3 (3¼-3½-3-3¼)" apart and planning to have one more in neckband—6 (6-6-7-7) buttonholes total. Work even until 12 (12½-13-13½-14)" from beg.

Right Front: Right side facing, work on 47 (50-53-56-59) sts and leave rem sts on holder. Working on these sts only, work even for 4 (4½-5-5½-6)".

natural black angora was spun and then dyed black. The Shetland, obtained raw, was scoured, teased, carded, and spun. The Maine island fleece was scoured, dyed, teased, carded, and spun.

DYEING

dye types and sources: Telana dye from Cerulean Blue, scarlet; Craftsman's acid dye from The Ruggery, black.

process: The Merino and Shetland are used in their natural colors. The black angora, which appears gray in its natural state, was overdyed black with acid dye from Craftsman's dyes. See sweater 2, Novelty Yarn Pullover, for the acid dyeing technique. The yarn from Maine island fleece was already dyed red with Telana (see sweater 5, Island Fleece Pullover).

SPINNING TECHNIQUE: Merino: Sliding short draw. Island fleece: Supported long draw. Angora and Shetland: Sliding long draw.

YARN

weight: Worsted (5 stitches/inch).

yards per pound: Merino and angora, 1200; Shetland and Maine island, 870.

number of plies: 2.

singles t.p.i.: 5-7.

plying t.p.i.: 3-4.

Then, at neck edge, leave 12 (13-14-15-16) sts on holder for front of neck, then at same edge dec 1 st every other row 6 times. Work even on rem 29 (31-33-35-37) sts until 20 (21-22-23-24)" from beg or to total desired length. Leave sts on holder.

Back: Work on next 85 (91-97-103-109) sts until same length as front to shoulder. Work last row as follows: Work on 29 (31-33-35-37) sts, place marker, work on 27 (29-31-33-35) sts, place marker, work to end of row. Leave sts on holder.

Left Front: Work on remaining 47 (50-53-56-59) sts completing as for right front, reversing neck shaping.

Armhole Ribbing: Using the knitted seam method, join shoulder seams. With 16" circular needle and A, begin at underarm and pick up and k 80 (84-90-94-100) sts around armhole opening. Work around in k1, p1 rib for 1". Bind off all sts in rib.

Neckband: With smaller needle and A, right side facing, work across 12 (13-14-15-16) sts from right front holder, pick up and k 21 sts on side of neck, work across 27 (29-31-33-35) sts from back holder, pick up and k 21 sts on side of neck, work on 12 (13-14-15-16) sts from left front holder. Working back and forth, keep first and last 5 sts in Garter st and work on center 83 (87-91-95-99) sts in ribbing as for lower back for ½". Work last buttonhole, then work even until band is 1" wide. Bind off all sts in rib.

Finishing: Sew buttons opposite buttonholes.

□ = A
□ = B
☒ = C
■ = D

For all sizes, start at A, work to B, repeat from A to B across row, end at C

C B   A

FIBER
type and source: Shetland wool top from Silver Crown Farm.

characteristics: The fine-grade wool fiber is scoured and ready to spin. We chose a natural oatmeal color, which we overdyed. Fiber length is 4-5″.

preparation: After being dyed and dried, the fiber was pulled to a manageable size and spun.

DYEING
dye type and source: Cushing's Perfection all-fiber type dye, in Wood Rose.

process: The fiber was wound into 1-pound skeins, which were tied loosely in four places, wetted, and dyed. We used one package of dye for each pound of fiber. Use the same process as for acid dyes, described for sweater 2 (Novelty Yarn Pullover), since it is the acid dye component of this mixed dye that will be operating on the wool.

You can spin matching yarns in two weights to make a set of garments. Stitch patterns, modified to work at the different gauges, subtly complement each other.

A coordinated sweater set required a fiber which would work well at both sport and worsted weights (for vest and cardigan, respectively). Since we planned to use a Shetland lace stitch pattern, Shetland wool seemed ideal—especially when we acquired Shetland top in a lovely oatmeal shade which would give depth to our hand-dyed color.

We dyed the wool in the fleece, using an old rose color. We've mentioned Telana dyes as superior for evenness of dyeing and strength of color (see page 18). Those were *not* qualities we wanted in this sweater, feeling the results would be too "commercial" and not as distinctive, so we used Cushing dyes. These are union dyes, meaning they contain various types of dyes, one for animal fibers, one for vegetable fibers, and one or more for synthetic fibers. The final color of our dyed fleece has lots of subtle variation, from both the fleece and the dye.

Both pieces of the set use the same stitch pattern in different ways. Because this particular pattern changes the number of stitches in different rows, we have given three general sizes (35, 40, and 45) to avoid making life complicated. The vest, worked in the lighter yarn, uses the stitch as an all-over pattern. The cardigan, in worsted weight, seemed both warmer and more graceful worked primarily in stockinette with isolated sections of pattern.

The cardigan has set-in sleeves and the vest has shaped armholes. Both have V-neck shaping, with full-fashioned details.

Spinning the matching yarns of different weights was an exercise in spinning control. Rachael spun the fine yarn first, since it's easier to come up a size than go down one. You'll need to constantly check the weight of the yarn you are spinning. The two weights are hard to tell apart just by looking. It's easiest to distinguish them by taking a doubled strand of each and twisting it back on itself; the difference is easier to see with more plies to compare. The yarn did blossom considerably when it was washed, so be sure your samples produce the desired results after finishing.

Several other prepared fibers would work effectively in this garment set—the supplier also has marbled slivers and light gray top.

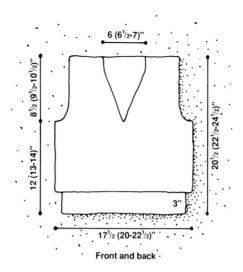

6 (6½-7)"

8½ (9½-10½)"

12 (13-14)"

20½ (22½-24½)"

3"

17½ (20-22½)"

Front and back

VEST

KNITTING INSTRUCTIONS

Instructions are for finished size 35". Changes for 40" and 45" are in parentheses.

Materials: Silver Crown Farm Shetland wool top, spun to sport weight: 8½ (10½-13) ounces or 985 (1215-1505) yards sport weight wool. One pair each size 3 and 5 needles or size needed to obtain correct gauge. One 16" size 3 circular needle.

Gauge: In Lace pattern with size 5 needles, 6 sts and 8 rows=1".

Stitches Used: *Stockinette stitch. Lace pattern (worked on 15 sts)—Row 1:* K2, yo, k1, yo, sl 1, k2 tog, psso, k3, k3 tog, yo, k1, yo, k2. *Row 2 and all wrong side rows:* Purl. *Row 3:* K2, yo, k3, yo, ssk, k1, k2 tog, yo, k3, yo, k2. *Row 5:* K2, yo, ssk, k1, k2 tog, yo, sl 1, k2 tog, psso, yo, ssk, k1, k2 tog, yo, k2. *Rows 7 & 9:* K2, (yo, ssk, k1, k2 tog, yo, k1) twice, k1. *Row 10:* As row 2. Repeat these 10 rows for pattern.

Note: Since the number of stitches increases to 17 on row 3, be sure to work your armhole and shoulder bind-offs after row 1, 5, 7, or 9 only. Take care also when working armhole and neck decreases to watch stitch counts.

Back: With smaller needles, cast on 97 (111-127) sts. Row 1: K1, *p1, k1. Row 2: P1, *k1, p1. Work these 2 rows until 3" from beginning, inc 8 (9-8) sts evenly in last row—105 (120-135) sts. Then, with larger needles, work across in Lace pattern for rest of back. At 12 (13-14)" from beginning, shape armhole: Bind off 7 sts at beg of next 2 rows, then work as follows starting with right side facing: Row 1: K1, ssk, work to last 3 sts, k2 tog, k1. Row 2: Purl. Repeat these 2 rows 7 times more. Work even on remaining 75 (90-105) sts until 8½ (9½-10½)" above armhole. Shape shoulders: Work across 20 (25-31) sts and leave on holder, work across next 35 (40-43) sts and leave on holder for back of neck, work across remaining sts and leave on holder.

Front: Work as for back, shaping armhole, AT THE SAME TIME, at 12 (14-15¾)" from beginning, shape neck: Divide work in half leaving center stitch on holder for sizes 35 and 45. Then, working on left side only with right side facing, and leaving remaining sts on holder, work to 3 sts before center, k2

SPINNING TECHNIQUE: Sliding short draw.
YARN
weight: Sport (6 stitches/inch) and worsted (5 stitches/inch).
yards per pound: Sport, 1850; worsted, 1050.
number of plies: 2.
singles t.p.i.: Sport, 8-10; worsted, 6.
plying t.p.i.: Sport, 5; worsted, 4.

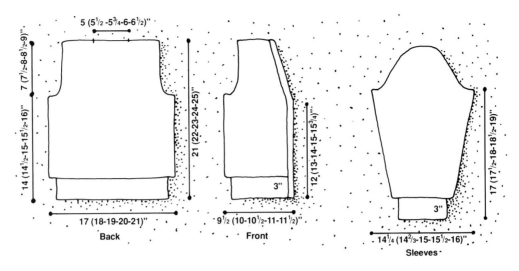

5 (5½-5¾-6-6½)"

7 (7½-8-8½-9)"

14 (14½-15-15½-16)"

21 (22-23-24-25)"

17 (18-19-20-21)"

Back

12 (13-14-15-15¾)"

3"

9½ (10-10½-11-11½)"

Front

17 (17½-18-18½-19)"

3"

14¼ (14⅔-15-15½-16)"

Sleeves

tog, k1. Turn, purl back. Repeat these 2 rows 16 (19-20) times more for neck shaping. Work even on remaining 20 (25-31) sts until same length as back to shoulder. Join shoulder sts to left back shoulder sts using the knitted seam method.

To complete other side, work neck decreases at beginning of right side rows as follows: K1, ssk. Work as for left side, reversing armhole and neck shapings. Once finished, join sts to right back shoulder sts using the knitted seam method.

Neckband: With circular needle, begin at left shoulder seam and pick up and k 57 sts along neck edge to center of V, pick up 1 st in center of V or knit stitch from holder, pick up and k 57 (56-57) sts along neck edge, then work across 35 (40-43) sts from back holder. Work around in k1, p1 rib on these 150 (154-158) sts keeping the center stitch of V knitted in every row and dec 1 st each side of this center stitch every row. Work even until band is 1" wide. Bind off all sts in rib.

Armhole Bands: Sew side seams to armhole. With circular needle and right side facing, attach yarn at underarm seam and pick up and k 114 (126-138) sts around armhole edge. Work around in k1, p1 rib for 1". Bind off all sts in rib.

CARDIGAN

KNITTING INSTRUCTIONS

Instructions are for finished size 35". Changes for 37", 39", 41", and 43" are in parentheses.

Materials: Silver Crown Farm Shetland wool top, spun to worsted weight: 15¼ (16¾-18-19½-21¼) ounces or 1000 (1100-1180-1280-1395) yards. One pair each size 3 and 5 needles or size needed to obtain correct gauge. Five (5-6-6-6) ⅝" buttons.

Gauge: In St st with size 5 needles, 5 sts and 7 rows = 1".

Stitches Used: *Stockinette stitch. Lace pattern (worked on 17 sts)—Row 1:* K2 tog, yo, (k1, yo) twice, sl 1, k2 tog, psso, k3, k3 tog, (yo, k1) twice, yo, ssk. *Row 2 and all wrong side rows:* P. *Row 3:* K2 tog, yo, k1, yo, k3, yo, ssk, k1, k2 tog, yo, k3, yo, k1, yo, ssk. *Row 5:* K2 tog, yo, k1, yo, ssk, k1, k2 tog, yo, sl 1, k2 tog, psso, yo, ssk, k1, k2 tog, yo, k1, yo, ssk. *Rows 7 & 9:* K2 tog, yo, k1, (yo, ssk, k1, k2 tog, yo, k1) twice, yo, ssk. *Row 10:* As row 2. Repeat these 10 rows for pattern.

Note: Work shoulder shaping only after row 2, 6, 8, or 10 since number of stitches increases after row 3 and is restored only on row 5.

Back: With smaller needles, cast on 81 (87-91-97-101) sts. Work ribbing as for vest for 3", inc 6 sts evenly in last row—87 (93-97-103-107) sts. Then, with larger needles, work across as follows: In St st on 12 (13-14-15-15) sts, in Lace pattern on 17 sts, in St st on 29 (33-35-39-43) sts, in Lace pattern on 17 sts, in St st on 12 (13-14-15-15) sts. Work as established for rest of back. AT THE SAME TIME, at 14 (14^1/$_2$-15-15^1/$_2$-16)" from beginning, shape armhole: Bind off 5 sts at beg of next 2 rows, then work as follows starting with right side facing: Row 1: K1, ssk, work to last 3 sts, k2 tog, k1. Row 2: Purl. Repeat these 2 rows 4 times more. Work even on remaining 67 (73-77-83-87) sts until 7 (7^1/$_2$-8-8^1/$_2$-9)" above armhole. Shape shoulders: Work across 21 (23-24-26-27) sts and leave on holder, work across next 25 (27-29-31-33) sts and leave on holder for back of neck, work across remaining sts and leave on holder.

Left Front: With smaller needles, cast on 41 (43-45-49-51) sts. Work in k1, p1 rib for 3", inc 3 (4-4-3-3) sts evenly in last row—44 (47-49-52-54) sts. Then, with larger needles, work across as follows: In St st on 12 (13-14-15-15) sts, in Lace pattern on 17 sts, in St st on 15 (17-18-20-22) sts. Work as established until 12 (13-14-15-15^3/$_4$)" from beginning. Shape neck: Right side facing, work across to last 3 sts, k2 tog, k1. Purl back. Repeat these 2 rows 12 (13-14-15-16) times more for neck shaping. AT THE SAME TIME, shape armhole as for back where required. Work even on remaining 21 (23-24-26-27) sts until same length as back to shoulder. Join shoulder sts to left back shoulder sts using the knitted seam method.

Right Front: Work as for left front, reversing pattern placement and armhole and neck shapings (work ssk instead of k2 tog at neck edge). Once finished, join sts to right back shoulder sts using the knitted seam method.

Sleeves: With smaller needles, cast on 40 (42-44-46-48) sts. Work in ribbing as for back for 3", inc 15 sts evenly in last row—55 (57-59-61-63) sts. Then, with larger needles, work across as follows: In St st on 19 (20-21-22-23) sts, in Lace pattern on center 17 sts, in St st on 19 (20-21-22-23) sts. Work as established for rest of sleeve, inc 1 st each end every $1^2/_3$ ($1^3/_4$-$1^3/_4$-$1^3/_4$-$1^3/_4$)" 8 times, working new sts in St st—71 (73-75-77-79) sts. Work even until 17 ($17^1/_2$ -18-$18^1/_2$-19)" from beginning, or desired length to underarm. Shape cap: Bind off 5 sts at beg of next 2 rows, then dec 1 st each end every other row until 25 sts remain. Bind off 3 sts at beg of next 6 rows. Bind off remaining 7 stitches.

Neckband: With smaller needles, begin at left shoulder seam and right side facing, pick up and k 48 sts along neck edge to point where neck shaping begins, then pick up and k 60 (65-70-75-80) sts to lower edge of front. Work in k1, p1 rib on these 108 (113-118-123-128) sts for 1". Bind off all sts in rib. To complete other side, right side facing, begin at lower right front edge and pick up and k 108 (113-118-123-128) sts along front edge as for first side, then work across 25 (27-29-31-33) sts from back holder. Work in k1, p1 rib on these 133 (140-147-154-161) sts for $^1/_2$" ending with a wrong-side row. For buttonholes, work across as follows on next right-side row: Work on 3 sts, then [yo, k2 tog, work on 12 (13-11-12-13) sts] 4 (4-5-5-5) times, yo, k2 tog, work to end of row. Work even until band is 1" wide. Bind off all sts in rib.

Finishing: Sew ends of front bands together at left shoulder. Set in sleeves at armhole openings. Sew underarm and side seams. Sew buttons opposite buttonholes.

FIBER

type and source: Cotswold fleece from Jones Sheep Farm.

characteristics: This medium-to-coarse, long fiber came in raw form.

preparation: The wool was lightly picked, scoured, teased, dyed, teased more completely, and carded, then pulled to a manageable size and spun.

DYEING

dye type and source. Telana dyes from Cerulean Blue, violet and magenta.

process: The scoured weight of wool was divided as follows: 8 ounces for violet, dyed with a 3% depth of shade solution (that is, 15 grams of dye were used); 14 ounces for plum, dyed with 1% depth of shade solutions of both magenta and violet (that is, 4 grams of magenta dye and 4 grams of violet dye were used); 10 ounces for pink, dyed with a 1% depth of shade solution of

(continued)

Knitted from side to side in colors which grade from light to dark, this sweater has a simple structure and a lot of impact.

Cotswold is not "average" wool. It's a medium to coarse fiber which always has more body and texture than run-of-the-mill wool, and can be brushed after a garment is finished to give a surface "fluff." Cotswold fleeces themselves vary a lot, from relatively fine and silky to very coarse. Some could be called "poor man's mohair."

This particular Cotswold fleece was the spinner's challenge and the knitter's dream. The locks were truly *locked* together—they couldn't be picked apart before they were washed. So into the water they went, and as they absorbed moisture they loosened up and could be pulled apart. The spinning also demanded extra attention. The effort, however, was worthwhile—the knitter thought the yarn was gorgeous and nice to work with.

We wanted visual impact in this sweater, a side-to-side structure, and colors which graded from light to dark. The clean, partially opened fiber was dyed in three colors; those colors were carded by themselves and in two additional blends, for a total of five colors. Hélène decided to work the colors together in a zigzag formation coordinated with the cuff-to-cuff construction. The use of stockinette stitch allows the color to carry the day.

There are many ways to modify this design concept. The dark colors could be in the central position, with light colors at the cuffs, or a selection of natural tones could be used. Different fibers in contrasting colors, all spun to the same weight, would be interesting.

KNITTING INSTRUCTIONS

Instructions are for finished size 36". Changes for sizes 38", 40", and 42" are in parentheses.

Materials: Jones Sheep Farm's Cotswold, spun to worsted weight: 2 ounces or 100 yards violet (A); $3\frac{1}{4}$ ($3\frac{1}{4}$-$3\frac{1}{2}$-$3\frac{1}{2}$) ounces or 165 (165-175-175) yards plum/violet (B); $2\frac{3}{4}$ (3-$3\frac{1}{2}$-4) ounces or 140 (150-175-200) yards plum (C); 5 ($5\frac{1}{4}$-$5\frac{1}{2}$-$5\frac{3}{4}$) ounces or 250 (260-275-285) yards pink/plum (D); $2\frac{3}{4}$ ($3\frac{1}{2}$-4-5) ounces or 135 (175-200-250) yards pink (E). One pair each size 4 and 6 needles, one 16" size 4 and one each 24" size 4 and 6 circular needles, or size to obtain correct gauge.

Gauge: In St st with size 6 needles, 5 sts and 6 rows=1".

Note: Pullover is worked from cuff to cuff.

Begin at Cuff: With smaller needles and A, cast on 41 (43-45-47) sts. Work in k1, p1 rib for 3", inc 14 sts evenly in last row—55 (57-59-61) sts. Then, with larger needles, begin St st and follow color sequence, and inc 1 st each end every 6 (6-5-5) rows 13 (14-16-17) times—81 (85-91-95) sts. Color sequence: Work 12 rows with A (about 2")—59 (61-63-65) sts. Work chart on next 10 rows working "dots" with A and "Xs" with B and keeping increases as established. Work 7" with B, then work chart as before positioning evenly across row and working "dots" with B and "Xs" with C. With C work until 18 (18½-18-19½)" from beg.

magenta (that is, 3 grams of dye were used). Follow the Telana dye instructions that we gave for sweater 5 (Island Fleece Pullover).
BLENDING: The dyed fiber was divided as follows for carding:
    4 ounces of violet
    4 ounces each of plum and violet, carded together
    6 ounces of plum
    4 ounces each of plum and pink, carded together
    6 ounces of pink
SPINNING TECHNIQUE: Supported long draw.
YARN
weight: Worsted (5 stitches/inch).
yards per pound: 800.
number of plies: 2.
singles t.p.i.: 4-5.
plying t.p.i.: 2-3.

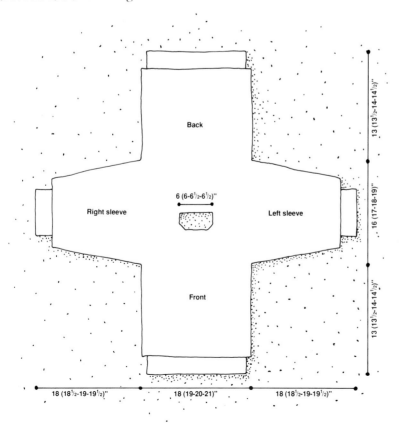

Back

13 (13½-14-14½)"

6 (6-6½-6½)"

Right sleeve

Left sleeve

16 (17-18-19)"

Front

13 (13½-14-14½)"

18 (18½-19-19½)"   18 (19-20-21)"   18 (18½-19-19½)"

Body: With C and larger 24" circular needle, cast on 50 (53-55-58) sts at beg of next 2 rows—181 (191-201-211) sts. Work 1" with C. Work chart on next 10 rows working "dots" with C and "Xs" with D. Work D for 3", then work chart working "dots" with D and "Xs" with E. Work with E to center of pullover—27 (28-29-30)" from beg. AT THE SAME TIME, at 6 (6$\frac{1}{2}$-6$\frac{3}{4}$-7$\frac{1}{4}$)" from body cast-on row, divide work: Right side facing, work on 90 (95-100-105) sts and leave remaining sts on holder for front. Work on this side only keeping color pattern as instructed above for 3 (3-3$\frac{1}{4}$-3$\frac{1}{4}$)" or 27 (28-29-30)" from beg. Place marker. You are now at halfway point. To complete back of neck, reverse color pattern working for 3 (3-3$\frac{1}{4}$-3$\frac{1}{4}$)" more. Leave sts on holder for back. To complete front and front neck shaping, bind off first 10 sts from front holder, then working on this side only, dec 1 st at neck edge every row 4 times. Work even until 3 (3-3$\frac{1}{4}$-3$\frac{1}{4}$)" from beg of neck shaping and place marker. Work other half of neck, reversing color placement and shaping. Wrong side facing, work across sts from needle then sts from back holder. Complete pullover, reversing color pattern, and body and sleeve shapings. Be sure to change needle size when working sleeve cuff. Bind off loosely.

Neckband: With smaller 16" circular needle and E, pick up and k 80 (80-84-84) sts around neck opening. Work around in k1, p1 rib for 1". Bind off in rib.

Lower Band: Sew side and underarm seams. With smaller 24" circular needle and D, pick up and k 168 (178-188-198) sts along lower edge. Work around in k1, p1 rib for 3". Bind off loosely using larger needle.

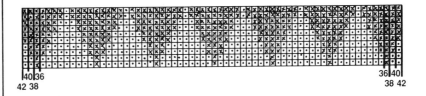

40 36 36 40
42 38 38 42

Note: This chart indicates first placement on sleeve only. It does not illustrate increases and subsequent chart placements.

15 SILK AND WOOL PULLOVER

The yarn on this sweater was designed first. Hélène asked for a yarn "without a dominant color, but small dashes of other colors that did not connect." The fiber spun very nicely, and the dominant idea of the sweater became *softness*. This is another fiber which blossoms considerably when it is finished, so samples are important for achieving the correct spinning size.

Rachael used very pale, "sherbet" colors, painting them onto the skeins of spun yarn. The dyes were mixed with dye paste, which is a mixture of a thickener and the chemicals that make the dye chemically bond to the fiber. Using this dye feels like painting with smooth tapioca. Rachael arranged the skeins in triangular shapes so the dye colors would not bleed into each other.

Then Hélène finished designing the sweater. It's important to knit this one to exact gauge for several reasons. The yarn drapes a lot and needs to be held in check or the sweater will droop. In addition, because of the construction technique the sleeves will be either too short or too long if the gauge is off.

The sweater is made from back to front. As a result, the cables are worked "upside down." You'll notice that the front has a few more stitches than the back to allow for the draw-in of the cable. To echo the "dashes" of color in the yarn, Hélène added short textured lines of garter stitch to the fabric.

KNITTING INSTRUCTIONS

Instructions are for size 34¹/₂". Changes for sizes 38" and 42" are in parentheses.

Materials: Gerald Whitaker silk and wool top, spun to light worsted weight: 13¹/₄ (15³/₄-19) ounces or 950 (1135-1365) yards. One pair each size 4 and 6 needles or size to obtain correct gauge. One 29" size 6 circular needle. One 15" size 4 circular needle. One cable needle (cn). One size F crochet hook. Two ¹/₂" buttons.

Gauge: In Dash st with size 6 needles, 5.5 sts and 8 rows=1".

FIBER

type and source: Silk-and-wool top from Gerald Whitaker.

characteristics: Fine grade fibers, 2-3″ long.

preparation: This commercially prepared fiber needed only to be pulled to a manageable size for spinning.

SPINNING TECHNIQUE: Sliding long draw.

YARN

weight: Light worsted (5.5 stitches/inch).

yards per pound: 1150.

number of plies: 2.

singles t.p.i.: 6.

plying t.p.i.: 3-4.

DYEING

dye type and source: Procion H fiber-reactive dye in colors called acid yellow and acid red, and Paste SH from PRO Chemical.

process: The skeined yarn was wetted in warm water and detergent and then rinsed. A flat surface was covered with white paper, and the skeins were arranged on it in triangular shapes. Mere pinches of

(continued)

Soft in fiber, color, and construction, this garment excels in comfort, but looks like a million—you can have it all!

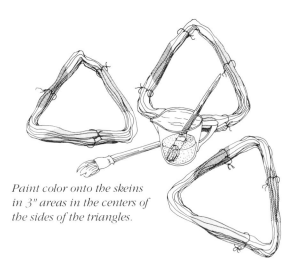

Paint color onto the skeins in 3" areas in the centers of the sides of the triangles.

Stitches Used: *Stockinette stitch. Cable (worked on 16 sts)—Row 1:* P2, k2, p2, k4, p2, k2, p2. *Row 2:* K2, p2, k2, p4, k2, p2, k2. *Rows 3 & 5:* As row 1. *Rows 4 & 6:* As row 2. *Row 7:* P2, sl 4 to cn and hold in back, k2, then p2 and k2 from cn; sl 2 to cn, hold in front, k2, p2, then, k2 from cn; p2. *Rows 8 & 10:* As row 2. *Rows 9 & 11:* As row 1. *Rows 12–16:* K. Repeat these 16 rows for pattern. *Dash stitch—Rows 1–6:* Work in St st. *Row 7:* P5, *k5, p5; rep from *. *Row 8:* Purl. *Rows 9-14:* Work in St st. *Row 15:* K5, *p5, k5; rep from *. *Row 16:* Purl. Repeat these 16 rows for pattern.

Note: Sweater is worked from back to front.

Back: With smaller needles, cast on 87 (97-107) sts. Row 1: K1, *p1, k1. Row 2: P1, *k1, p1. Repeat these 2 rows for 3", inc 8 sts evenly in last row—95 (105-115) sts. With larger needles, begin working Dash st from back. AT THE SAME TIME, at 10 (11-12)" from beg, begin shaping armhole and sleeves: Cast on 6 (5-5) sts at beg of next 16 (18-20) rows, then 4 (3-3) sts at beg of next 16 (26-30) rows. Be sure to work Dash st on new sts and change to larger circular needle when sts get too crowded. Place markers each end of row. Work even on obtained 255 (273-305) sts until 20 (22-24)" from beg. Place markers each end of row.

Front: Right side facing, work across 113 (120-135) sts and leave remaining sts on holder. Then, working on this side only, work even for 1¹/₂", then at neck edge inc 1 st every other row 5 times ending ready to work a wrong side row, leave these 118 (125-140) sts on holder. To complete other side, leave first 29 (33-35) sts on holder for back of neck, then work as for first side, ending ready to work a wrong-side row. Work across sts on needle, cast on 22 (26-28) sts, work across sts from holder. Next row, work on these 258 (276-308) sts as follows: Work in Dash st as established on 121 (130-146) sts, in Cable pattern on center 16 sts, in Dash st to end of row. Work even until same length as between first and second sleeve markers on back.

Begin Armhole Shaping: Bind off 4 (3-3) sts at beg of next 16 (26-30) rows, then 6 (5-5) sts at beg of next 16 (18-20) rows, changing to shorter straight needles when needed. Continue as established on remaining 98 (108-118) sts until same length as back to neck less 3", dec 11 sts evenly in last row—87 (97-107) sts. Then, with smaller needles, work in rib as for back. Using larger needle, bind off all sts in rib.

dye were mixed with dye paste; acid red and acid yellow produced the pink and yellow shades, and the two colors were combined to make the melon shade. Colors were painted onto the yarn in 3″ areas in the centers of the sides of the triangle (see diagram). The dye was allowed to set for 20 minutes, then the skeins were rinsed and placed in 180° F water for an additional 30 minutes before being allowed to hang dry.

Cuffs: With smaller needles and right side facing, pick up and k 45 (47-49) sts. Wrong side facing, work in rib as for back, beginning with row 2. Work as established for 3". With larger needle, bind off all sts in rib.

Collar: With smaller circular needle and right side facing, start at right edge of front and pick up and k 19 (23-25) sts on front edge, pick up and k 17 sts on right side of neck, work across 29 (33-35) sts from back holder, pick up and k 17 sts on left side of neck, then pick up and k 19 (23-25) sts on front edge working behind sts first picked up. Work back and forth in rib on these 101 (113-119) sts binding off 2 sts at beg of next 10 (12-12) rows. Next row, bind off all sts in rib. Attach yarn at front neck edge. With crochet hook, work 1 row single crochet along entire neck opening making 2 buttonloops on front diagonal edge.

Finishing: Sew underarm and side seams. Sew buttons opposite buttonholes.

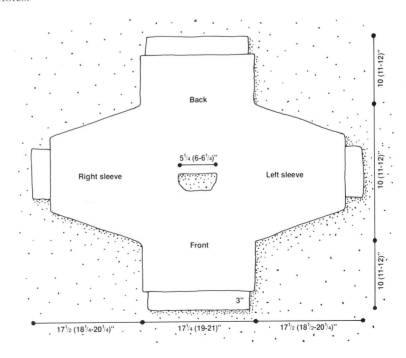

FIBER

type and source: Romney/Perendale top from R. H. Lindsay.

characteristics: A medium-grade fiber with a length of 4-5″.

preparation: The wool was skeined, tied loosely, wetted, dyed, rinsed, and dried. Then it was split into four sections lengthwise. These were spun in succession.

DYEING

dye type and source: Acid dye. We used Craftsman's dyes from The Ruggery in black, blue, violet, and green.

process: The wetted skeins were placed in a large dyepot around a gallon container that had been placed in the middle of the dyepot. Water containing $1/2$ cup of white vinegar was added to just cover the wool. Dye powders were mixed into stock solutions of 1 tablespoon dye in a pint of boiling water, with separate solutions for each of the

(continued)

A peacock-inspired quartet of colors, applied to singles with a technique easy enough for beginners, makes the perfect yarn for a quick vest you'll wear frequently.

This completely prepared Romney/Perendale blend is a good fiber for beginners—or for any spinner in a hurry. It can be spun hard or soft, to be lofty or dense, as a heavy or fine yarn. It's inexpensive and takes dye beautifully and with reasonably predictable results. You'll be able to get a vest up to size 40/42 out of a single pound, which happens to be the capacity of the average dyepot.

We used one of the "rainbow" dyeing techniques, where a number of colors are applied in one dyepot, to get our color variations. We couldn't resist trying other combinations of four colors. Let our names for the sets of colors spur your imagination: spring lavender, blue emerald, pink champagne, red sunrise, stormy mauve. The vest *could* be knitted in a solid color, of course, or in blended fibers.

Dye was applied to the unspun top. We skeined and loosely tied it, then arranged it around a core (gallon jar) in the dyepot. This kept it in order so we could have more control over the placement of colors. The dye was poured on (see diagram) and the fiber wasn't stirred.

To produce a relatively even mix of colors throughout the garment, we did *not* pull the top to size as usual. Instead, Rachael split the top longitudinally into four more-or-less equal lengths, then spun these in sequence. How to split that long supply of fiber? Banish all cats and children (especially those carrying lollipops) from the living room. Secure the space. Unwind the top around the room. Begin by splitting in half, moving around as necessary. On your second pass, split each half again in half. This time you can wind the sections into manageable balls as you go.

To save on spinning time: a single strand in light, bulky weight goes quickly.

Rainbow-dyed yarn tends to make unintentional horizontal stripes when you knit with it, but there are tricks to minimize this effect. Hélène has accomplished this by calling for a combination of garter stitch and ribs. The "stripiness" will be more obvious in your swatch than it is in the full-width garment. If the "stripes" in your actual fabric are too noticeable, you can use two balls of yarn and knit alternate rows (or pairs of rows) with them. We didn't need to do this.

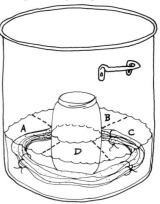

KNITTING INSTRUCTIONS

Instructions are for finished size 35". Changes for sizes 38" and 41" are in parentheses.

Materials: R. H. Lindsay's Romney/Perendale top, spun to light bulky weight: 13$\frac{1}{2}$ (15-17) ounces or 465 (515-585) yards. One pair each size 8 and 10$\frac{1}{2}$ needles or size needed to obtain correct gauge. One 16" size 8 circular needle.

Gauge: In Pattern st with size 10$\frac{1}{2}$ needles, 4 sts = 1".

Stitches Used: *Stockinette stitch. Pattern stitch—Rows 1 & 2:* K. *Rows 3 & 4:* K1, p1.

Back: With smaller needles, cast on 60 (66-72) sts. Work in k1, p1 rib for 3$\frac{1}{2}$", inc 10 sts evenly in last row to 70 (76-82) sts. Then, with larger needles, work in Pattern st for rest of back. At 21 (22-23)" from beginning, work first 24 (26-28) sts and leave on holder, work across next 22 (24-26) sts and leave on holder for back of neck, work on remaining sts and leave on holder.

Pocket Lining: With larger needles, cast on 16 sts. Work in St st for 4". Leave sts on holder.

Front: Work as for back until 13$\frac{1}{2}$ (14$\frac{1}{2}$-15$\frac{1}{2}$)" from beginning. Right side facing, work across 16 sts, work in k1, p1 rib on next 16 sts, and work to end of row as established. Work even for 1". Then, right side facing, work across 16 sts, bind off next 16 sts, work to end of row. Next row, work to bound-off sts from previous row, then, in Pattern, work across the 16 sts of pocket lining from holder and complete row. Work even until 17 (18-19)" from beginning. Right side facing, work across 29 (31-33) sts, leave remaining sts on holder. Working on this side only, dec 1 st at neck edge every other row 5 times. Work even on remaining 24 (26-28) sts until same length as back to shoulder. Leave sts on holder.

To complete other side, leave center 12 (14-16) sts on holder for front of neck and work on remaining sts as for first side, reversing neck shaping.

Neckband: Join shoulders using the knitted seam method. With circular needle, and right side facing, pick up and k 18 sts on side of neck, work

colors listed above. From these stock solutions, small amounts of four colors were mixed as follows:

- #1: 4 tsp. green and 3 tsp. black
- #2: 4 tsp. blue and 3 tsp. black
- #3: 12 tsp. violet
- #4: 4 tsp. green.

Dyes were poured onto the wool, maintaining quadrants of color areas as shown in the diagram. Each color area was pushed up and down with a dowel to encourage dye saturation but the dyepot was not stirred. The dyepot was simmered for 30 minutes, then the fiber was rinsed and dried.

SPINNING TECHNIQUE: Supported long draw.

YARN

weight: Light bulky (4 stitches/inch).

yards per pound: 550.

number of plies: 1.

singles t.p.i.: 3-4.

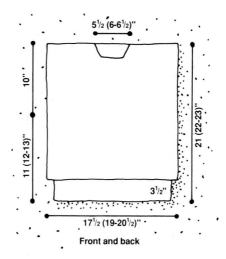

5½ (6-6½)"

10"

11 (12-13)"

21 (22-23)"

3½"

17½ (19-20½)"

Front and back

across 12 (14-16) sts from front holder, pick up and k 18 sts on side of neck, work across 22 (24-26) sts from back holder. Work around on these 70 (74-78) sts in k1, p1 rib for 1". Bind off in rib.

Armhole Bands: Measure 10" on each side of shoulder seams and place markers on armhole edge. Sew side seams to markers. With circular needle, and right side facing, pick up and k 86 sts around armhole opening. Work in k1, p1 rib for 1". Bind off firmly in rib.

Finishing: Slip stitch pocket lining in place.

A gallon jar helps keep the skeins in order, so you can control color placement.

17 MERINO CARDIGAN

As a fiber, Rachael could live with Merino "forever" and Hélène described this yarn as "creamy." Merino is noted as being difficult to spin, but a great deal of the challenge in working with very fine wools is in preparing the raw fleece properly. This Merino came as clean, combed top, which neatly sidestepped the entire issue of preparation. Although this fine wool is a bit tricky for a beginner, one can quickly adjust to working with its softness. This project is not out of reach for a serious beginning spinner. If you'd like to set a goal which can be accomplished a little more quickly, you can eliminate the sleeves, add ribbed sleeve bands, and make a buttoned vest instead of a cardigan. The yarn is perfect for any garment worn close to the skin, or for those who are sensitive to other wools. Because dyeing the unspun fiber caused felting, it was necessary to dye in-the-yarn. The yarn is smooth, because the sweater's primary interest comes from color and pattern. Like some of the other finer wools, Merino blossoms noticeably when it is washed; the samples for yarn size need to be finished completely.

The yarn took the dye very evenly but in a lively manner. There are very subtle color changes which enrich the sweater as you get closer; these are not completely apparent in the photograph. After the yarn was dyed in teal and light blue, two slightly unusual colors to use together, Hélène designed several pattern swatches; she and Rachael agreed on the second possibility.

Because of the elaborate color patterning, a classic sweater shape was chosen. It was updated with a low V-neckline and dropped shoulder shaping.

KNITTING INSTRUCTIONS

Instructions are for finished size 35". Changes for sizes 37", 39", 41", and 43" are in parentheses.

Materials: R. H. Lindsay's Merino top, spun to light worsted weight: 11½ (12½-13¼-14-15) ounces or 720 (780-825-875-940) yards teal (A), 7 (7½-8-8¾-9¼) ounces or 440 (470-500-545-580) yards light blue (B). One pair each size 6 and 8 needles or size to obtain correct gauge. Four ⅝" buttons.

FIBER
type and source: Merino top from R. H. Lindsay.
characteristics: This fine-grade wool has a fiber length of 2-3″.
preparation: The commercially prepared fiber was pulled to a manageable size for spinning.
SPINNING TECHNIQUE: Sliding short draw.
YARN
weight: Light worsted (5¼ stitches/inch).
yards per pound: 1000.
number of plies: 2.
singles t.p.i.: 6-7.
plying t.p.i.: 3-4.
DYEING
dye type and source: Cushing's Perfection dye in a color called Copenhagen Blue; and Craftsman's acid dye from The Ruggery in yellow, magenta, turquoise, and blue.
process: 8.5 ounces of finished yarn were dyed with one package of Cushing's Copenhagen
(continued)

Merino offers the ultimate woolen softness to spinner, knitter, and recipient: by working with Merino in commercially prepared form, even a relatively inexperienced spinner can enjoy its benefits.

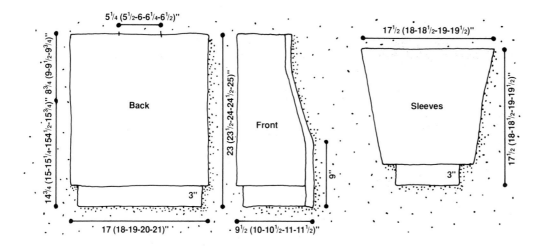

Schematic measurements:

Back: 5¼ (5½-6-6¼-6½)"; 8¾ (9-9½-9¾)"; 14¾ (15-15½-15¾)"; 17 (18-19-20-21)"; 3"

Front: 23 (23½-24-24½-25)"; 9½ (10-10½-11-11½)"; 9"

Sleeves: 17½ (18-18½-19-19½)"; 17½ (18-18½-19-19½)"; 3"

Gauge: In Color pattern with size 8 needles, 5.25 sts=1".

Stitches Used: *Stockinette stitch.*

Back: With smaller needles and A, cast on 81 (87-91-97-103) sts. Row 1: K1, *p1, k1. Row 2: P1, *k1, p1. Work these 2 rows for 3", inc 8 sts evenly in last row—89 (95-99-105-111) sts. Then, with larger needles and in St st, work following chart repeating until 23 (23½-24-24½-25)" from beginning or desired length to shoulders. Shape shoulders: Work across 31 (33-34-36-38) sts, leave on holder, work across next 27 (29-31-33-35) sts and leave on holder for back of neck, work across remaining sts and leave on holder.

Left Front: With smaller needles and A, cast on 41 (43-45-49-51) sts. Work in ribbing as for lower back for 3", inc 4 (5-5-4-5) sts evenly in last row—45 (48-50-53-56) sts. Then, with larger needles, in St st, work across, following chart as for back. At 9" from beginning, shape neck: Right side facing, work to last 3 sts, k2 tog, k1. Purl back. Repeat these 2 rows 13 (14-15-16-17) times more. Work even on remaining 31 (33-34-36-38) sts until same length as back to shoulder. Leave sts on holder.

Right Front: Work as for left front working neck shaping at beginning of right side rows as follows: K1, ssk, work to end of row.

Sleeves: With smaller needles and A, cast on 41 (43-45-47-49) sts. Work in ribbing as for lower back for 3", inc 22 sts evenly in last row—63 (65-67-69-71) sts. Then, with larger needles, in St st, work across, following chart and being careful to center pattern. AT THE SAME TIME, inc 1 st each end every 1 (¾-1-1-1)" 14 (15-15-15-16) times, working new sts in Color pattern. Work even on obtained 91 (95-97-99-103) sts until 17½ (18-18½-19-19½)" from beginning or to total desired length. Bind off all sts.

Neckband: Join shoulder seams using the knitted seam method. With smaller needles and A, begin at left shoulder seam and pick up and k 77 (79-83-85-87) sts to point where neck shaping begins, then pick up 40 sts to lower edge. Work in ribbing on these 117 (119-123-125-127) sts for 1". Bind off in rib. To complete other side, begin at lower right front edge, and pick up and k 40 sts to point where neck shaping begins, pick up and k 76 (78-82-84-86) sts to shoulder seam and work across 27 (29-31-33-35) sts from back holder. Work in ribbing on these 143 (147-153-157-161) sts for ½". Right side

Blue. For the 13 ounces of teal, the following quantities of 1% stock solutions (made with 1 tablespoon of dye in a pint of boiling water) were added to the dyepot:
 25 ml yellow
 25 ml magenta
 300 ml turquoise
 400 ml blue.
For both dyes, follow the process for acid dye that we described for sweater 2 (Novelty Yarn Pullover).

facing, work as follows: Work on 3 sts, (yo, k2 tog, work on 10 sts) 3 times, yo, k2 tog, work to end of row. Work even until band is 1" wide. Bind off all sts in rib.

Finishing: Sew ends of band together at left shoulder seam. Measure $9\frac{1}{2}$ ($9\frac{3}{4}$-10-$10\frac{1}{4}$-$10\frac{1}{2}$)" on each side of shoulder seams and place markers on armhole edge. Set in sleeves between markers, stretching slightly to fit. Sew underarm and side seams. Sew buttons opposite buttonholes.

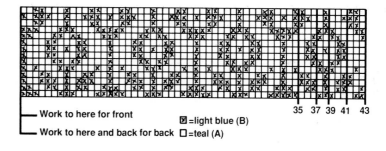

— **Work to here for front**   ☒ =light blue (B)
— **Work to here and back for back**   ☐ =teal (A)

35 37 39 41 43

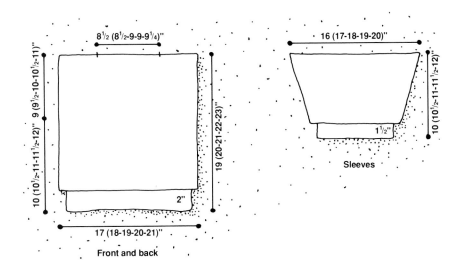

8½ (8½-9-9-9¼)"

9 (9½-10-10½-11)"

10 (10½-11-11½-12)"

19 (20-21-22-23)"

2"

17 (18-19-20-21)"

Front and back

16 (17-18-19-20)"

10 (10½-11-11½-12)"

1½"

Sleeves

FIBER

type and source: Silk-and-linen top from The Silk Tree.

characteristics: A blend of fine bleached linen and fine silk, with a fiber length of about 2".

preparation: The commercially prepared fiber was pulled to a manageable size for spinning.

SPINNING TECHNIQUE: Supported long draw.

PLYING AND YARN DESIGN

The singles were divided and plied as follows:

7 ounces as simple 2-ply.

17 ounces as 2-ply with nub added every 12". The nub was made by allowing one strand to wind back and forth over one spot on the other strand (see diagram).

YARN

weight: Sport (5.5 stitches/inch).

yards per pound: Smooth, 960; nubby, 860.

number of plies: 2.

singles t.p.i.: 7.

plying t.p.i.: 3-4.

This unusual combination of fibers works up into a sweater with both presence and appeal. You can dress it up or down, and you'll want to wear it frequently.

Hélène is particularly pleased with this type of sweater, with its comfortable, easy shape and bright colors—although the design would work well in a similarly shiny natural-colored yarn as well. The silk here contributes softness while the linen adds body. This mix of soft and crisp fibers has excellent sheen.

Because both linen and silk are present, fiber-reactive dyes work best. These dyes with an alkaline solution are excellent for dyeing plant fibers, and silk will also take the same dye. The fiber took the dye very well. The unusual combination of chocolate, turquoise, and magenta includes a solid background color and two accents.

An interesting but fairly common thing happened in the dyepot. The yarn that we dyed black came out chocolate brown. We were pleased with it and we used it as our background color, but don't be surprised if dye colors don't come out quite like you expected. The age of the dye, the age or growing conditions of the fiber, the amount of chlorine in your water, and other factors will affect dye colors.

There are two distinct yarns in this sweater, one a smooth chocolate strand, the other a textured, multicolored strand. When Rachael was spinning, she decided to add nubs to the multicolored yarn, to emphasize the light-reflective qualities of the fibers. "Pulling to a manageable size," a routine mentioned for most of the sweaters in this book, becomes particularly important with a blend of diverse fibers like this one. If you simply spin the fibers as they come, you can end up with a palm full of the shorter fibers at the end of your spinning session. The long ones draw in easily, leaving the shorties behind. Pulling helps control the distribution of the varying fibers and, with a smaller amount in your hand, it's more likely that you'll be able to keep both types of fiber feeding evenly into your yarn.

Since so much is going on in the yarn's color and texture, a simple style became essential. Dropped shoulder shaping, a boatneck, and three-quarter-length sleeves make this a classic pullover for all seasons. The multicolored sections of the sweater are worked in stockinette since the nubs add sufficient texture, and the solid-colored sections are in ribbing or garter stitch.

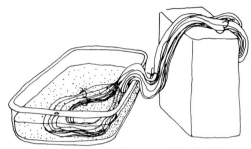

Leave two-thirds of the skein out of each dyebath.

KNITTING INSTRUCTIONS

Instructions are for finished size 34". Changes for sizes 36", 38", 40", and 42" are in parentheses.

Materials: Silk Tree's silk and linen blended top, spun to sport weight: 10 (11½-13-14-15½) ounces or 540 (620-700-755-833) yards nubby yarn (A), 4½ (5-5½-6-6½) ounces or 270 (300-330-360-390) yards smooth yarn (B). One pair each size 2 and 4 needles or size to obtain correct gauge.

Gauge: In St st with size 4 needles, 5.5 sts=1".

Stitches Used: *Stockinette stitch. Garter stitch.*

Note: When working with this textured yarn, purposely keep the nubs to the front of work for best effect.

Back: With smaller needles and B, cast on 79 (85-91-97-101) sts. Work in k1, p1 rib for 2", inc 14 sts evenly in last row—93 (99-105-111-115) sts. Then, with larger needles, begin Color pattern as follows: Work 3" with A in St st, then 6 rows with B in Garter st. Repeat this sequence for rest of back. Work even until 18 (19-20-21-22)" from beg. Then, work with B in Garter st for 1". Next row, work on 23 (26-28-31-32) sts and leave on holder, bind off next 47 (47-49-49-51) sts, work to end of row and leave these sts on holder.

Front: Work as for back.

Sleeves: With smaller needles and B, cast on 53 (55-57-59-61) sts. Work in k1, p1 rib for 1½", inc 16 (17-18-19-20) sts evenly in last row—69 (72-75-78-81) sts. Then, with larger needles and A, work in same Color pattern as for back. AT THE SAME TIME, inc 1 st each end every ¾ (¾-¾-¾-⅔)" 10 (11-12-13-14) times—89 (94-98-104-109) sts. Work even until 10 (10½-11-11½-12)" from beg. Bind off all sts loosely.

Finishing: Join shoulders using the knitted seam method. Measure 9 (9½-10-10½-11)" on each side of shoulder seams and place markers on armhole edge. Set in sleeves between markers, stretching slightly to fit. Sew underarm and side seams.

DYEING

dye type and source: Procion H fiber-reactive dyes in black, blue, turquoise, and magenta, soda from PRO Chemical, and uniodized salt from a grocery store.

process: The skein of smooth yarn was dyed in black dye. The multicolored nubby yarn was dyed in three separate colors, with one-third of the skein placed in each (see diagram). Some overlap of dye areas was allowed, so white areas would not occur. Dye powders were mixed into stock solutions of 1 tablespoon dye in a pint of boiling water, with separate solutions for each of the colors listed above. One-third of the presoaked skein was placed in a dyepot containing *3 tsp. black* (see illustration) and left for one hour, with occasional very gentle stirring. Then another third of the skein was placed in a second dyebath containing *1 tsp. blue and 1 tsp. turquoise,* for another hour. The final third of the skein was placed in a third dyebath containing *1 tsp. blue and 1 tsp. magenta,* for another hour. The skein was rinsed and hung to dry.

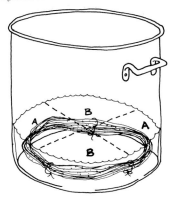

Apply the two colors in opposite quarters of the dyebath.

FIBER

type and source: Welsh Mountain wool top from R. H. Lindsay.

characteristics: A medium-to-coarse wool with wiry guard hairs; fiber length is 7".

preparation: The top was made into large skeins and loosely tied in four places. It was wetted in warm water, dyed, rinsed, dried, and pulled to a manageable size for spinning.

DYEING

dye type and source: acid dyes. We used PRO acid dyes from PRO Chemical in blue, black, and red.

process: Dye powders were mixed into stock solutions of 1 tablespoon dye in a pint of boiling water, with separate solutions for each of the colors listed above. Denim blue was used on 17 ounces of the fiber, using the acid dyeing technique we described for sweater 2 (Novelty Yarn Pullover) (recipe: 1 c. blue and 1/3 c. black). Denim blue (recipe: 3/4 c. blue and 1/4 c. black) and red (recipe: 3/4 c. red and 1/4 black) were used on an additional 13 ounces of fiber, in a single dyepot with the rainbow dyeing method, as follows: A gallon container was placed in the center of the pot and the skeined fiber was arranged around it, then wet with a vinegar and water solution as was done for sweater

(continued)

Our first encounter with Welsh Mountain fleece was in a vest like the variegated one made of Romney/Perendale blend. It's much too coarse a fiber to be used next to the body, but fascinating to dye and work with because it contains guard hairs, or *kemp*, which accept the dye much less willingly than the fleece in general. This gives interesting tonal variations.

The kemp also produces a slightly "hairy" and rustic texture in both yarn and fabric, which is like a haze on the surface. Other fibers, like mohair, produce fuzzy surfaces, but they're so dominant they have to be compensated for in the sweater's design. Welsh Mountain's halo is subtle and allows a great deal of design freedom.

We wanted an "average" sweater with set-in sleeves. We wanted it to fit a wide range of sizes, have an optional V-neckline or a crewneck, and be open to modification in many directions. Using the format of this sweater, you can change the stitch pattern, use solid yarn, make stripes, and so forth—as long as you remember to get your gauge right.

Since the fiber added all the texture we could use, we decided to work in stockinette and play with color. We dyed pale colors to blend with the kempy halo, but it would be interesting to dye dark shades and see what happens to a fabric made with higher contrast. One could do a whole study of how one breed's fleece interacts with various dyes. We did find that the colors we got weren't quite what we expected (we were looking for a denim-like blue and got one with a slight green tone). Because of our approach to this series of sweaters, that was fine. To refine our technique, we would need to experiment further with each individual fiber. But we wanted to make sweaters, not take *more* notes, and since we did like the results, we adapted to them.

We dyed just over half of our fiber in a solid "denim" blue. The remainder we colored in a single pot using the same blue and a red. We spun each type separately. Then we made a solid blue 2-ply yarn for the ribbing, to unify our design, and plied the variegated yarn with a solid blue strand for a 2-ply which changed slowly from one color to the next. This subtle change of color throughout the garment eliminates the striping effect usually apparent in yarns made this way.

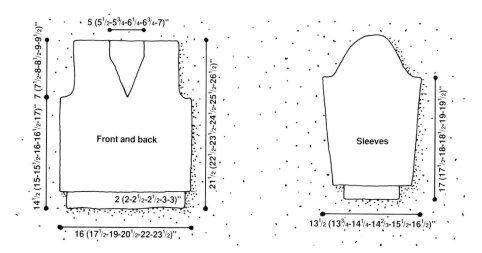

Front and back — 5 (5¹/₂-5³/₄-6¹/₄-6³/₄-7)"

7 (7¹/₂-8-8¹/₂-9-9¹/₂)"

14¹/₂ (15-15¹/₂-16-16¹/₂-17)"

21¹/₂ (22¹/₂-23¹/₂-24¹/₂-25¹/₂-26¹/₂)"

2 (2-2¹/₂-2¹/₂-3-3)"

16 (17¹/₂-19-20¹/₂-22-23¹/₂)"

Sleeves

17 (17¹/₂-18-18¹/₂-19-19¹/₂)"

13¹/₂ (13³/₄-14¹/₄-14²/₃-15¹/₂-16¹/₂)"

When it came time to knit, we used circular needles for the body. This keeps the front and back unified, since the broad color shifts occur evenly.

KNITTING INSTRUCTIONS

Instructions are for finished size 32". Changes for sizes 35", 38", 41", 44", and 47" are in parentheses.

Materials: R. H. Lindsay's Welsh Mountain top, spun to worsted weight: 2 (2¹/₂-3-3-4-4) ounces or 90 (110-130-130-175-175) yards solid color (A), 12¹/₂ (14¹/₂-15¹/₂-17-19-21) ounces or 550 (635-680-745-830-920) yards variegated color (B). One each 24" size 5 and 7 circular needles or size to obtain correct gauge. One pair straight needles each in sizes 5 and 7.

Gauge: In St st with size 7 needles, 4.5 sts = 1".

Stitches Used: *Stockinette stitch.*

Note: Body is worked in one piece to armhole.

Body: With smaller circular needle and A, cast on 132 (146-160-172-186-200) sts. Placing marker at beginning of rnd and taking care not to twist row of sts, work around in k1, p1 rib for 2 (2-2¹/₂-2¹/₂-3-3)", inc 12 sts evenly in last rnd—144 (158-172-184-198-212) sts. Then, with B and larger circular needle, work in the rnd in St st until 14¹/₂ (15-15¹/₂-16-16¹/₂-17)" from beginning. Divide for armholes: Starting at marker, bind off 5 sts, work on 62 (69-76-82-89-96) sts, bind off next 10 sts, work on 62 (69-76-82-89-96) sts, bind off next 5 sts. Place last group of sts worked on holder for front.

Back: Attach yarn at start of row for back and continue on these sts working back and forth in St st, shaping armholes as follows: Bind off 1 st each end every other row 5 times. Work even on remaining 52 (59-66-72-79-86) sts until 7 (7¹/₂-8-8¹/₂-9-9¹/₂)" from armhole. Shape shoulders: Bind off 5 (6-7-7-8-9) sts at beg of next 4 rows, then 5 (5-6-8-8-9) sts at beg of next 2 rows. Leave remaining 22 (25-26-28-31-32) sts on holder for back of neck.

Front: Working armhole shaping as for back, work neck shaping as follows: For sizes 32, 38, 41, 47, work to center of piece. For sizes 35 and 44, work to

15, the Variegated Vest. Denim blue dye was poured over two opposite quarters of fiber, and red dye over the remaining quarters. A little poking with a dowel encouraged dye penetration and some color blending, but no stirring was done. Each dyepot was simmered for 30 minutes, then the fibers were rinsed and allowed to hang dry.
SPINNING TECHNIQUE: Supported long draw.
YARN
weight: Worsted (4¹/₂ stitches/inch).
yards per pound: 700.
number of plies: 2; blue plied with blue for ribbing; blue plied with variegated for body.
singles t.p.i.: 6.
plying t.p.i.: 3-4.

Some wools, like Welsh Mountain, have so much character they can be challenging to work with. But the limitations are also strengths, as demonstrated in this pullover.

center stitch and leave it on a holder. Then, for all sizes, working both sides at the same time using separate skeins of yarn (try to select strands of yarn that will keep the continuity of color similar on both sides of neck), dec 1 st at neck edge every $1/2$" 11 (12-13-14-15-16) times. Work even on remaining 15 (17-20-22-24-27) sts until same length as back to shoulder. Shape shoulders as for back.

Sleeves: With smaller straight needles and A, cast on 35 (37-39-41-43-45) sts. Work back and forth as follows: Row 1: K1, *p1, k1; rep from *. Row 2: P1, *k1, p1; rep from *. Work as established until 2 (2-$2^1/2$-$2^1/2$-3-3)" from beg, inc 11 sts evenly in last row—46 (48-50-52-54-56) sts. Then, with larger straight needles and B, work back and forth in St st, inc 1 st each end every 2 (2-2-$2^1/4$-$1^3/4$-$1^3/4$)" 7 (7-7-7-8-9) times—60 (62-64-66-70-74) sts. Work even until 17 ($17^1/2$-18-$18^1/2$-19-$19^1/2$)" from beginning or desired length to underarm. Shape armholes and cap: Bind off 5 sts at beg of next 2 rows, then dec 1 st each end every other row until 22 sts remain. Then, bind off 2 sts at beg of next 6 rows. Bind off rem 10 sts.

Neckband: Sew shoulder seams. With smaller circular needle and A, begin at left shoulder seam and pick up and k 36 (38-40-43-45-47) sts on left neck edge, knit one stitch in center of V, pick up and k 37 (38-41-44-45-48) sts on right side of neck, work across 22 (25-26-28-31-32) sts from back holder. Work around in k1, p1 rib on these 96 (102-108-116-122-128) sts for 1" keeping stitch in center of V knitted on all rows and dec 1 st each side of this center stitch every row. Bind off all sts in rib.

Finishing: Sew sleeve seams and set in at armhole openings.

Crew Neck Option:

Additional Material Required: One 16" size 5 circular needle. Yarn quantities should be about the same.

Follow directions for back and sleeves as above.

Front: Work to underarms. Work as for V-neck version, omitting instructions for neck shaping at this point. Instead, work even until $4^1/2$ (5-$5^1/2$-$5^1/2$-6-$6^1/2$)" above armholes. Then, right side facing, work across 20 (22-25-27-29-32) sts, attach a 2nd skein of yarn, work across next 12 (15-16-18-21-22) sts and leave on holder for front of neck, work on remaining sts. Then, working both sides at the same time, dec 1 st at neck edge every other row 5 times. Work even on remaining 15 (17-20-22-24-27) sts until same length as back to shoulders. Shape as for back.

Neckband: Sew shoulder seams using the knitted seam method. Then, with 16" circular needle and A, beginning at left shoulder seam, pick up and k 14 (14-14-16-16-16) sts on side of neck, work across 12 (15-16-18-21-22) sts from front holder, pick up and k 14 (14-14-16-16-16) sts on side of neck, work across 22 (25-26-28-31-32) sts from back holder. Work around in k1, p1 rib on these 62 (68-70-78-84-86) sts for 1". Bind off in rib.

Finishing: As for V-neck version.

FIBER

type and source: Medium-grade mohair top from Gerald H. Whitaker.

characteristics: Very long and slippery fibers with gorgeous luster.

preparation: The top was divided evenly by weight into three portions and was wound into large, loose skeins, each of which was tied in four places. One skein was left natural. The remaining two skeins were dyed as indicated below. When dry, the top was pulled apart into 8" lengths. The fiber was drum carded, with one length of each of the three colors in each batt. The batts were pulled to a manageable size for spinning.

DYEING

dye type and source: PRO acid dyes from PRO Chemical in blue, yellow, and black.

(continued)

Although there are commercial mohair yarns, there's no exact equivalent for handspun mohair. Dyed in three closely related soft greens, the fiber in this design is shiny, forthright, and irresistible.

Handspun mohair is often not as light and fluffy as commercially spun mohair—it's got a feel of its own and can be a challenge to design with. The stitch shape is a little rounder than with a wool yarn, and some pattern stitches (like the combination of ribs and cable found here) need to be blocked carefully. Hélène says mohair has "lots of life," and "a mind of its own." The knitter dearly loved working on this sweater because of its texture and color.

More sampling than usual went into the design of this sweater to get all the elements just right—samples were made for both dye mixes and design ideas. Initially, Rachael dyed three different gradations of sea green, spun them separately, and plied them all together. This looked stripy, and the effect detracted from the fiber's natural sheen and the color's quality. When she carded natural fiber and several shades of green together and spun them, the resulting heathery sea-green yarn had a subtle, rich, and pleasing depth. It was spun evenly to allow some stitch detail to show.

When it was time to sample stitches, a true cable looked sloppy. The resulting successful choice produced the illusion of a cable from a traveling diagonal rib. Because individual stitches are more rounded than usual, a standard knit one/purl one rib doesn't look right—the stitches open up into Os and look loose. A twisted rib works much better.

Since mohair is not a fiber many people can wear close to their skin, a cardigan seemed to be a logical style choice. Classic shaping, with set-in sleeves, was chosen, although the body length was designed to be slightly shorter than usual. When knitting, plan to spend extra time measuring pieces and calculating your gauge.

This design could be worked in other fibers. In most of these cases, regular ribbing could be used.

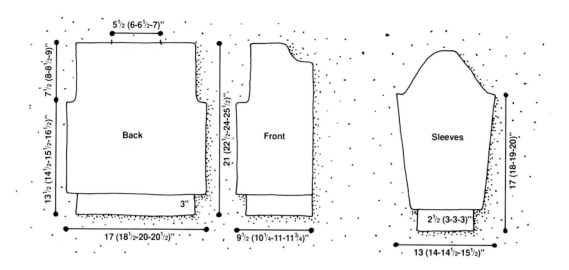

KNITTING INSTRUCTIONS

Instructions are for size 35". Changes for sizes 38", 41", and 44" are in parentheses.

Materials: Gerald Whitaker's top, spun to light bulky weight: 20½ (23½-26¾-30) ounces or 680 (780-885-995) yards 100% mohair. One pair each size 8 and 10½ needles or size to obtain correct gauge. Seven (7-8-8) buttons.

Gauge: In Pattern st, slightly blocked with size 10½ needles, 4.5 sts = 1".

Stitches Used: *Garter stitch. Raised rib—Row 1:* K1 through back loop (k1b), *p1, k1b; rep from *. *Row 2:* P1 through back loop (p1b), *k1, p1b; rep from *. *Pattern stitch—Row 1 and all wrong side rows:* K2, p1b, k2, *p5, k2, p1b, k2; rep from *. *Row 2:* P2, k1b, p2, *skip one stitch, k next stitch through back, slip first st as if to purl, and drop 2nd stitch from needle (left cross=LC), k3, p2, k1b, p2; rep from *. *Row 4:* P2, k1b, p2, *k1, LC, k2, p2, k1b, p2; rep from *. *Row 6:* P2, k1b, p2, *k2, LC, k1, p2, k1b, p2; rep from *. *Row 8:* P2, k1b, p2, *k3, LC, p2, k1b, p2; rep from *. Repeat these 8 rows for pattern.

Note: Model garment is shown with 6 buttonholes. We recommend that you follow instructions and make 7 (7-8-8) buttonholes.

Back: With smaller needles, cast on 71 (77-85-91) sts. Work in Raised rib for 3", ending with a right-side row and inc 6 sts evenly in last row—77 (83-91-97) sts. Then, with larger needles, wrong side facing, begin working as follows: St st on 6 (9-3-6) sts, Pattern st on center 65 (65-85-85) sts, St st to end of row. Work as established until 13½ (14½-15½-16½)" from beg or desired length to underarm. Shape armholes: Bind off 5 sts at beg of next 2 rows, then dec 1 st each end every other row 4 (4-3-4) times. Work on remaining 59 (65-75-79) sts as established. Work even until 7½ (8-8½-9)" above armhole. Shape shoulders: Right side facing, work on 17 (19-23-24) sts, leave on holder, work on 25 (27-29-31) sts and leave on holder for back of neck, work on remaining sts and leave on holder.

Right Front: With smaller needles, cast on 40 (42-46-50) sts. Working in Garter st on first 5 sts and in Raised rib on remaining sts, work even for 1 (1-1-¾)". Make first buttonhole as follows: Right side facing, work 2 sts, yo, work 2 sts tog, work 1 st, work to end of row as established. Work even until 3" from beginning, end with a right-side row and inc 3 (4-4-3) sts in last row

process: Dye powders were mixed into stock solutions of 1 tablespoon dye in a pint of boiling water, with separate solutions for each of the colors listed above. Two of the three skeins of top were dyed in separate dyebaths, containing the following amounts of stock solutions:
   #1, light sea green: 3 tsp. blue, 1 tsp. yellow, ½ tsp. black
   #2, medium sea green: 12 tsp. blue, 4 tsp. yellow, 2 tsp. black
The third skein was left natural. Use the acid dye method that we used for the Novelty Yarn Pullover, sweater 2.
SPINNING TECHNIQUE: Supported long draw.
YARN
weight: Light bulky (4.5 stitches/inch).
yards per pound: 530.
number of plies: 3.
singles t.p.i.: 8-10.
plying t.p.i.: 4.

(do not make increases in first 5 sts on row—buttonhole band)— 43 (46-50-53) sts. On next wrong-side row, work as follows: St st on 6 (9-3-6) sts, Pattern st on next 32 (32-42-42) sts (end with a "p5, k2" sequence—do not work p1b, k2 that follows), Garter st on last 5 sts. Work keeping pattern as established working 5 (5-6-6) more buttonholes spaced 3 ($3^{1}/_{4}$-3-$3^{1}/_{4}$)" apart in center of band and planning to have one more in center of neck bank [7 (7-8-8) buttonholes total]. At same length as back to armholes, shape as for back— 34 (37-42-44) sts. Then work even until 5 ($5^{1}/_{2}$-6-$6^{1}/_{2}$)" above armholes. Shape neck: At neck edge, leave 12 (13-14-15) sts on holder for front of neck, then at same edge, dec 1 st every other row 5 times. Work even on remaining 17 (19-23-24) sts until same length as back to shoulders. Leave on holder.

Left Front: Work as for right front, reversing pattern placement and omitting buttonholes.

Sleeves: With smaller needles, cast on 37 (39-41-43) sts. Work in Raised rib for $2^{1}/_{2}$ (3-3-3)" ending with a right-side row, and inc 8 (10-12-14) sts evenly in last row—45 (49-53-57) sts. Then, wrong side facing, with larger needles, work across as follows: In St st on 0 (2-4-1) sts, in Pattern st on center 45 (45-45-55) sts, in St st to end of row. Work as established, inc 1 st each end every 2 (2-$2^{1}/_{2}$-$2^{3}/_{4}$)" 7 (7-6-6) times, working new sts in St st. Work even on obtained 59 (63-65-69) sts until 17 (18-19-20)" from beginning, or desired length to underarms. Shape cap: Bind off 5 sts at beg of next 2 rows, then dec 1 st each end every other row until 19 sts remain. Bind off 3 sts at beg of next 4 rows, bind off remaining 7 sts.

Neckband: Join shoulders using the knitted seam method. With smaller needles, work across 12 (13-14-15) sts from right front holder, pick up and k 13 sts on side of neck, work across 25 (27-29-31) sts from back holder, pick up and k 13 sts from left side of neck, work across 12 (13-14-15) sts from left front holder. Work back and forth on these 75 (79-83-87) sts keeping first and last 5 sts in Garter st and working on center sts in Raised rib for $^{1}/_{2}$", make last buttonhole, work even until band is 1" wide. Bind off all sts.

Finishing: Before assembling further, pieces need to be blocked carefully. Pin on towel to dimensions listed on schematics, and steam to size using a damp cloth and warm iron. Let dry. Set in sleeves at armhole openings. Sew underarm and side seams. Sew buttons opposite buttonholes.

FIBER
type and source: Wool top from Brown Sheep.

characteristics: Medium-to-fine-grade wool with a great deal of crimp.

preparation: The white was pulled to a manageable size and spun. The leaf color was dyed, carded, pulled, and spun. The motif colors were dyed in 1-ounce quantities, carded and blended to produce the intermediate colors, pulled, and spun. The extra carding was necessary after dyeing to open up the fibers for easy spinning. Spinning oil was also used.

DYEING
dye type and source: PRO acid dyes from PRO Chemical.

process: Stock solutions were mixed at 3% strength (3 tablespoons of dye powder

(continued)

Nine hand-dyed colors were blended to produce a palette of twenty hues; fourteen ultimately found their way into the full glory of this design. For a more subtle garment, the leafy background can be used as an all-over pattern, without the parrot.

There are two sweaters lurking in this design, one quite flashy and the other more sedate. While we're fond of the parrot (and so are our kids), this garment can be knitted with just the leaf pattern throughout. If you're not working with the parrot, you can make the leaves in two colors of green, or rust tones, or a number of color variations. To alter the effect of the parrot, you could work it with a complete change of palette to softer colors. In any case, the background colors should be significantly more muted than those in the parrot.

The sweater instructions are for only one size, 44", because there are more than 20 stitches in the leaf repeat and the parrot chart is so large. The easiest way to produce a smaller size is to spin a lighter-weight yarn which will knit up at a smaller gauge.

Since we began with the idea of a sweater with a picture, we selected a smooth, mid-range wool that would not compete with the colors and design. Working from 9 basic hand-dyed colors, Rachael blended and spun 20 colors, of which Hélène used 14 in her final design. Because the processed fleece became very dry after it had been dyed, Rachel resorted to the use of spinning oil. Various oils can be used for this purpose. Be sure to use something that washes out easily, and check the smell—some specially formulated oils smell a lot like petroleum and are not particularly pleasant to work with. Olive oil is one of the old standbys. To apply oil, spray it onto carded batts and let them sit for a little while to absorb it.

A technique called *Navajo plying*, in which a 3-ply yarn is produced from a single strand, works well when you've got small amounts of a lot of colors to deal with. Each color requires only one bobbin, and everything comes out even.

Because both leaf pattern and parrot are relatively complex, we chose a basic pullover with minimal shaping. In order to minimize breaks in the leaf pattern and keep the color stranding reasonably easy, the front and back of the sweater were knit at the same time. Work proceeded back and forth, with one side seam left open and joined later.

The chart for this sweater—even with the leaf pattern alone—is just irregular enough that the pattern won't run along in your head, so you'll need to stay close to the chart. To keep our place, we drew a

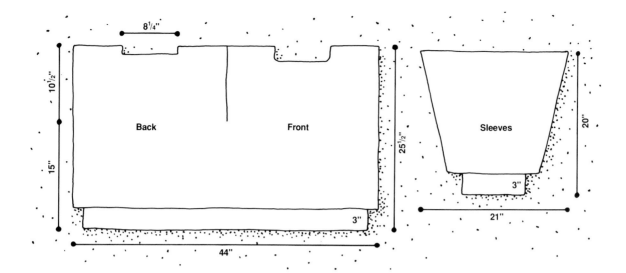

red line down the columns between the background repeats and used a magnetic board with a marking strip, made primarily for cross-stitchers. Because keeping track of the leaf pattern while shaping the sleeves would be crazy-making, Rachael suggested the checkerboard pattern in that area.

KNITTING INSTRUCTIONS

Instructions are for finished size 44" only, due to the nature of the graphed pattern. We suggest you alter your yarn weight to obtain a tighter gauge if a smaller size is desired.

Materials: Brown Sheep wool top, spun to light bulky weight: $17\frac{1}{2}$ ounces or 790 yards white (A), $11\frac{1}{2}$ ounces or 520 yards light green (B). For bird: 9 yards red brown, 8 yards red, 2 yards bright yellow, 7 yards gold, 10 yards orange red, 5 yards orange, 5 yards charcoal, 5 yards purple, 5 yards purple blue, 5 yards blue, 3 yards teal, 3 yards yellow green. One each 24" size 7 and 9 circular needles or size to obtain correct gauge. One pair straight needles in each of same sizes. One 16" size 7 circular needle.

Gauge: In St st with size 9 needle, 4.33 sts=1" or 13 sts=3".

Stitches Used: *Stockinette stitch.*

Note: Body is worked back and forth in one piece to armhole with only one side seam at left.

Body: With smaller 24" circular needle and A, cast on 173 sts. Row 1: K1, *p1, k1. Row 2: P1, *k1, p1. Work in this manner for 3", inc 18 sts in last row—191 sts. Then, follow chart 1 placing marker at side seam (after 96th st) and in between leaf motifs to help in following chart. Work even until 15" from beginning.

Divide for Armholes: Right side facing, work across 96 sts and leave remaining sts on holder. Work even on this side only until $23\frac{1}{2}$" from beg.

Neck Shaping: Right side facing, work on 32 sts and leave remaining sts on holder. Work on this side only binding off 1 st at neck edge every other row

dissolved in 1 pint of boiling water). The following amounts of these solutions were used, on 1 ounce of fiber each:
   #1, red: 4 tsp. red
   #2, orange: 1 tsp. yellow, $\frac{1}{8}$ tsp. red
   #3, yellow: $1\frac{1}{2}$ tsp. yellow
   #4, green: 2 tsp. yellow, $\frac{1}{2}$ tsp. blue
   #5, dark avocado: 6 tsp. yellow, $1\frac{1}{2}$ tsp. blue, $\frac{1}{2}$ tsp. red
   #6, teal: 4 tsp. turquoise, 4 tsp. blue
   #7, royal blue: 4 tsp. blue, 1 tsp. turquoise
   #8, brown: 1 tsp. each of blue, black, and yellow, $\frac{1}{4}$ tsp. red
   #9, charcoal: 2 tsp. black
Use the acid dye technique that we used for sweater 2 (Novelty Yarn Pullover). Carding and blending the dyed fleece, alone or in pairs of colors, produced approximately 20 colors to choose from for the motif. Colors selected were: *white (undyed), light green (leaf color), red, bright yellow, gold (yellow + orange), orange red (red + orange), orange, charcoal, purple (royal + red), purple blue (more royal + less red), blue (royal), teal, yellow green (yellow + green), red brown (red + brown).*

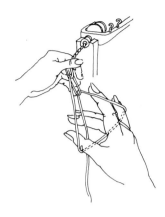

SPINNING TECHNIQUE: Supported long draw; Navajo plying. To Navajo ply, begin by tying one strand of yarn to the bobbin's leader. Make a loop from the strand and hold it in place with one hand. Let the other hand hold the loop open and reach through it to bring up the strand to be plied. (This is like crocheting a chain with big loops.) As you treadle, the three strands in each section of yarn will be twisted together and drawn onto the bobbin.

YARN
weight: Light bulky (4.33 stitches/inch).
yards per pound: 720.
number of plies: 3.
singles t.p.i.: 8.
plying t.p.i.: 3.

2 times. Work even on remaining 30 sts until $25^{1}/_{2}$" from beginning. Leave sts on holder.

To complete other side of front, leave center 32 sts on holder for front of neck and work on remaining sts completing as for first side. Leave sts on holder.

Back Yoke: Right side facing, work across sts on back holder casting on 1 st at beginning of row. Work on these 96 sts continuing chart pattern until $24^{1}/_{2}$" from beginning. Right side facing, work on 30 sts, leave remaining sts on holder. Work on this side only for 1". Leave sts on holder. Leave center 36 sts on holder for back of neck and work on remaining sts for 1". Leave on holder.

Neckband: Join shoulder seams using the knitted seam method. Then, with smaller circular needle and A, begin at left shoulder seam, and pick up and k 9 sts on side of neck, work across 32 sts from front holder, pick up and k 14 sts on side of neck, work across 36 sts from back holder, pick up and k 5 sts on side of back neck. Work around in k1, p1 rib on these 96 sts for 1". Bind off all sts in rib.

Sleeves: With smaller straight needles and A, cat on 39 sts. Work in rib as for lower back for 3", inc 19 sts evenly in last row—58 sts. Then, with larger straight needles, work in St st following chart 2. AT THE SAME TIME, inc 1 st each end every $^{3}/_{4}$" 2 times, then every 1" 14 times—90 sts. Work in a "one stitch A, one stitch B" pattern alternating every row on new sts for rest of sleeve. At 20" from beginning, bind off all sts.

Finishing: Sew side seam leaving a $10^{1}/_{2}$" opening for sleeve. Sew underarm sleeve seams and set in at armhole openings.

Chart 1

Repeat this section across back to shoulders

Key to color code

☐ white
☒ light green
☑ red
◙ bright yellow
⊞ gold
▯ orange red
◪ orange
■ charcoal
⊡ purple
◘ purple blue
⊟ blue
Ⓥ teal
◿ yellow green
◧ red brown

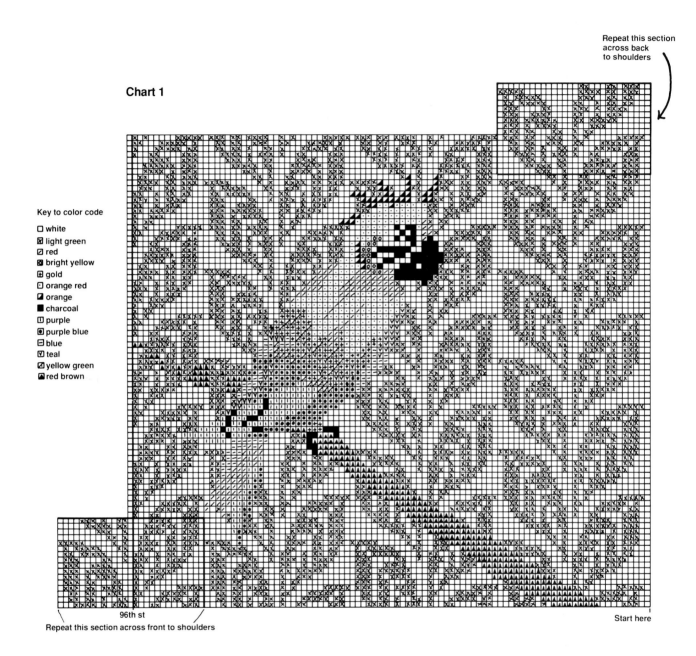

96th st

Repeat this section across front to shoulders

Start here

Chart 2

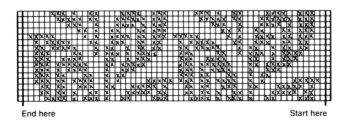

End here

Start here

118

FIBER

type and source: Raw Finn wool from The Spinners Hill Shop.

characteristics: Quite fine, with varied fiber length. Brown and white fleece were blended to produce a warm gray.

preparation: The wool was scoured, teased, and carded. Individual batts were carded with a ratio of 3 parts white to 1 part brown. Batts were then pulled and spun in two weights. Some of the skeins were left natural and others were dyed.

DYEING

dye type and source: PRO acid dye from PRO Chemical in blue, black, turquoise, and yellow.

process: After 3% stock solutions of dye were mixed (3 T dye powder to 1 pint boiling water), the following amounts of dye were used for the associated quantities of wool:

  #1, navy: 1 c. blue and 1/2 c. black—1 ounce worsted weight and 11 ounces sport weight

  #2, green: 4 tsp. yellow, 4 tsp. turquoise, 2 tsp. blue—1 ounce worsted weight

The acid dye process is described in the section on sweater 2 (Novelty Yarn Pullover).

(continued)

For an outdoor vest which would be extremely warm without being excessively bulky, we chose a soft, lofty fiber and a two-layer construction. This required that Rachael spin a worsted weight yarn (for the outer layer) and a sport weight yarn (for the lining). This is an early fall project, not a summer one—since the layers are worked in sequence and attached to each other, the knitter ends up with a lapful of wool which at the last moment comes together into a compact and comfortable garment. The completed lining is joined to the outer layer with crocheted vertical lines, which become part of the plaid pattern. Our raw wool from Finn sheep was very springy and crimpy. It came in various lengths and textures, and needed to be carefully blended in the carding to produce a uniform supply. Because of the extra attention in the carding, the spinning went reasonably well despite these differences. We mixed white and brown wool, at a 3-to-1 ratio, to produce a warm gray. Some of this we left natural, and some we overdyed into soft blue and green. The design would also look good in red, blue, and a cooler gray. For additional warmth, the lining yarn could incorporate some angora.

Our yarn was soft, lightweight, and bouncy. As usual when spinning and working with two closely related weights of yarn, telling the weights apart requires the "twist test" (see page 81). The yarn blossoms when washed; this contributed significantly to the feel of the finished fabric.

This vest consumes a lot of yarn. We ran out of the sport weight, but that turned into a blessing. There's a lot of ribbing (worked in double layers in the sport weight yarn), and we ran out on the lining. When we saw this was about to happen, we took apart the lining section and reworked it on much larger needles, with a larger gauge. This wound up being beneficial, because the vest is sufficiently heavy as it is.

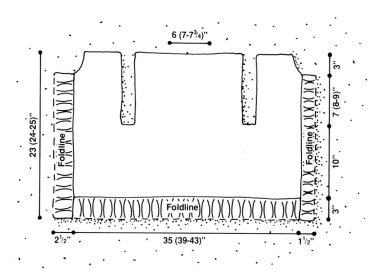

6 (7-7³/₄)"

23 (24-25)"

Foldline

Foldline

7 (8-9)"

3"

10"

3"

Foldline

2½"

35 (39-43)"

1½"

KNITTING INSTRUCTIONS

Instructions are for finished size 38". Changes for sizes 42" and 46" are in parentheses.

Materials: Spinner's Hill Shop's Finn fleece, spun to sport and worsted weights: 11¼ (12³/₄-14⅓) ounces or 700 (800-895) yards blue sport weight yarn (A), 11 (12³/₄-14³/₄) ounces or 515 (600-690) yards beige worsted weight yarn (B), 1¼ (1⅓-1²/₃) ounces or 60 (65-75) yards blue worsted weight yarn (C), ²/₃ (³/₄-1) ounces or 30 (35-45) yards green worsted weight yarn (D). One each 24" size 4, 8, and 11 circular needles or sizes to obtain correct gauges. Six clasp closures. One crochet hook size G.

Gauge: In St st with size 8 needle and B, 4.25 sts = 1". In St st with size 11 needles and A, 3 sts = 1".

Stitches Used: *Stockinette stitch.*

Note: Ribs are worked 2 times the desired length, then folded in half to inside. Vest is worked in one piece to armholes. Lining is worked once outside is done, starting from rib cast-on row.

Body: With size 4 circular needle and A , cast on 175 (197-219) sts. Row 1: K1, *p1, k1. Row 2: P1, *k1, p1. Repeat these 2 rows until 6" from beginning, dec 26 (32-36) sts evenly in last row—149 (165-183) sts. Then, right side facing, with size 8 circular needle and B, work in Color pattern as follows: Work 16 rows B, 2 rows D, 2 rows B, 2 rows C. Repeat these 22 rows for rest of piece. AT THE SAME TIME, work as follows: Row 1: K9 (2-11) sts, *p1, k9; rep from * 14 (16-16) times, p0 (1-1), k0 (2-11) sts. Row 2: K on k, p on p. Work as established in st and Color pattern indicated. At 10" above rib, divide for armholes as follows: Work on 28 (32-37) sts, bind off next 10 sts for armhole, work on 73 (81-89) sts, bind off next 10 sts for armhole, work on remaining sts.

First Front: Next row, work on first group of sts and leave remaining sts on holder. Work on this side only until 7 (8-9)" from beg. Bind off 0 (2-5) sts at neck edge, then dec 1 st at same edge every other row 4 times. Work even on remaining 24 (26-28) sts until 10 (11-12)" above armholes. Leave sts on holder.

SPINNING TECHNIQUE: Supported long draw.
YARN
weight: Sport (worked on large needles at 3 stitches/inch) and worsted (4.25 stitches/inch).
yards per pound: Sport, 1000; worsted, 750.
number of plies: 2.
singles t.p.i.: Sport, 6-8; worsted, 5.
plying t.p.i.: Sport, 4; worsted, 2-3.

This nifty vest is constructed in two layers and stitched together with vertical lines which become part of its pattern—warm!

120

Back: Work across center 73 (81-89) sts from holder and work even on these sts for 10 (11-12)". Next row, work on 24 (26-28) sts and leave on holder, bind off next 25 (29-33) sts for back of neck, work to end of row and leave on holder.

Second Front: Complete as for first side, reversing neck shaping. Assemble shoulders using the knitted seam method.

Lining: With size 11 needle and A, pick up and k 105 (117-129) sts on lower edge of ribbing. Work in St st in solid color for rest of lining. AT THE SAME TIME, at 10" above rib, divide for armholes: Right side facing, work on 21 (24-27) sts, bind off 6 sts for armhole, work on 51 (57-63) sts, bind off 6 sts for armhole, work to end of row.

First Front Lining: Wrong side facing, work on first group of sts and leave remaining sts on holder. Working on this side only, work even until 7 (8-9)" above armholes. Bind off 1 (2-3) sts at neck edge, then dec 1 st at same edge every other row 3 (4-4) times. Work even on remaining 17 (18-20) sts until 10 (11-12)" above armholes. Leave sts on holder.

Back Lining: Work on center 51 (57-63) sts from holder until 10 (11-12)" above armholes. Next row, work across 17 (18-20) sts, leave on holder, bind off next 17 (21-23) sts for back of neck, work to end of row and leave these sts on holder.

Second Front Lining: Complete as for first front, reversing neck shaping. Assemble shoulders using the knitted seam method.

Front Bands: With size 4 circular needle and A, pick up and k 109 (115-121) sts on left front edge for women, right for men, catching both inside and outside layers. Work in ribs as for lower edge for 5". Bind off in rib. With wrong side facing, fold band in half and slip stitch top and bottom edges shut. Fold right side out and slip stitch long edge to inside front. Work in same manner on other side for 3" and complete seams as for first side.

Neckband: Place markers on neck edge of front bands at $1/2$" from center edge on $1^1/2$" band, and at $1^1/2$" from center edge on $2^1/2$" band. With size 4 circular needle and A , pick up and k 83 (93-103) sts on neck between markers, catching in both layers. Work in rib for 2". Fold band in half and

122

sew ends shut on wrong side. Fold right-side out and slip stitch long edge to inside.

Armhole Bands: With size 4 circular needle and A, pick up and k 109 (121-131) sts around armhole openings beginning at underarm edge and catching in both layers. Work even for 2¼" in ribbing. Fold band in half to inside and slip stitch around armholes.

Finishing: With crochet hook and C, begin right above lower rib and work chain stitch in vertical purl-stitch ridges, catching in lining as you work up. Sew clasp closures in place.

23 DIAGONAL VEST

This is a project for people who have lots of little bags of fiber samples they don't know what to do with, and for those knitters who hate to cast on beginning stitches. The trick was in getting a variety of fibers carded together and in making them work. The lesson is that occasionally we need to cut loose—if the results are this good, conscientious abandon could happily occur more often!

There *is* a dominant fiber: 50% of the blend is ramie. The other 50% consists of camel, angora, Maine island fleece, and mohair. Rachael has found that blends like this succeed if one fiber makes up about half of the blend.

Some of our miscellaneous fibers had been dyed in colors unlikely to blend well—for example, the red of the Maine island fleece and the sea green of the mohair—but when combined in unequal amounts, the dash of sea green simply tempered the red's brilliance instead of cancelling it out. The final color displays shades of pink, honey, and green, with an overall pastel effect. The fibers' separate textures assert themselves in small ways, so the fabric has a gentle angora haze along with the ramie's sheen.

Thorough blending is essential. Once she had an idea of the color mix she wanted, Rachael divided hunks of the ramie into 16 parts on a large surface (a king-sized bed worked well). She took the remaining fibers and sprinkled some of each on every pile. After she carded each pile, she cross-carded the piles (half of this pile plus half of that pile, etc.). When she pulled the fiber to spinnable size, some fibers had to be watched to maintain a constant mix of fibers.

The swatch for this sweater was difficult to make predictions from, but forging ahead proved wise. The completed all-season vest is classically shaped but was constructed in interesting and fun ways. Only 6 stitches are cast on for the entire sweater—the shaping is done from there through increases, decreases, and pick-ups. The diagonal shaping is highlighted with simple cables which are echoed in the yoke and lower ribbing. The vest would also be successful in pure wool, and could be worked with stronger color variations.

FIBER

type and source: Combed white ramie (8 ounces) and natural camel (3 ounces) from Straw into Gold, white angora (2 ounces) from Wildhaere Farm, mohair ($3^1/_2$ ounces) from Gerald Whitaker (used dyed leftover from sweater 20), Maine island fleece ($2^3/_4$ ounces) from Wildwood (used dyed leftover from sweater 5).

characteristics: The ramie is shiny, smooth, and of varying length. The other fibers cover a wide range of lengths, sizes, luster, and crimp.

preparation: Fibers were mixed as noted above and drum carded, then cross-carded for further blending. Additional carding would have produced a more even mix of color and texture; samples may indicate that you want to do this. When pulling the fiber from a mixed-texture batt, be aware that some fibers will want to draw more easily than others. You have to actively pull the lazy fibers to maintain your consistency.

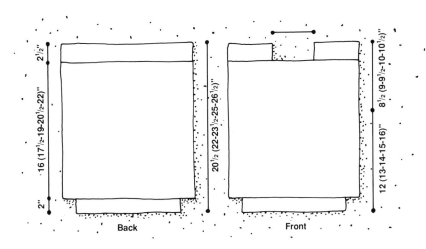

Back   Front

DYEING: No specific dyeing was planned for this project, because it used leftovers. However, if your mix of fibers doesn't please you, don't forget you can overdye.

SPINNING TECHNIQUE: Supported long draw.

YARN

weight: Light worsted (5 stitches/inch).

yards per pound: 920.

number of plies: 2.

singles t.p.i.: 6.

plying t.p.i.: 3.

KNITTING INSTRUCTIONS

Instructions are for finished size 32". Changes for sizes 35", 38", 41", and 44" are in parentheses.

Materials: Straw Into Gold's ramie, and fibers from various sources for blending, spun to light worsted weight: 9½ (11-12¾-14½-16½) ounces or 545 (630-735-835-950) yards. One pair each size 5 and 7 needles or size to obtain correct gauge. One 16" size 5 circular needle. One cable needle (cn).

Gauge: In St st with size 7 needles, 5 sts = 1".

Stitches Used: *Stockinette stitch. Reverse Stockinette stitch. Cable—Rows 1 & 3:* K4. *Row 2 and all wrong-side rows:* P4. *Row 5:* Slip 2 sts to cn, hold in back, k2, k2 from cn. *Row 6:* As row 2. Repeat these 6 rows for Cable. *Slipped rib (slyf)—Row 1:* K1. *Row 2:* Slip 1 with yarn in front. *Make One (M1)—*Pick up strand of yarn running between st just worked and next st, and knit in the back of it.

Note: Front and back main pieces are worked diagonally from corner to corner. Sts for lower ribbings and top yokes are then picked up.

Body: *(Make 2):* With larger needles, cast on 3 sts. *Row 1:* P1, k1, p1. *Row 2:* K1, slyf, k1. *Row 3:* P1, M1, k1, M1, p1. *Row 4:* K2, slyf, k2. *Row 5:* P1, M1, p1, k1, p1, M1, p1. *Row 6:* K3, slyf, k3. *Row 7:* K1, M1, p2, k1, p2, M1, k1. *Row 8:* P2, k2, slyf, p2, k2. *Row 9:* K1, M1, k1, p2, k1, p2, k1, M1, k1. *Row 10:* P3, k2, slyf, k2, p3. *Row 11:* K1, M1, k2, p2, k1, p2, k2, M1, k1. *Row 12:* P4, k2, slyf, k2, p4. *Row 13:* K1, M1, k3, p2, k1, p2, k3, M1, k1. *Row 14:* K1, p4, k2, slyf, k2, p4, k1. *Row 15:* P1, M1, k4, p2, k1, p2, k4, M1, p1. *Row 16:* K2, p4, k2, slyf, k2, p4, k2. *Row 17:* P1, M1, p1, k4, p2, k1, p2, k4, p1, M1, p1. *Row 18:* K3, p4, k2, slyf, k2, p4, k3. *Row 19:* K1, M1, p2, k4, p2, k1, p2, k4, p2, M1, k1. *Row 20:* P1, k3, p4, k2, slyf, k2, p4, k3, p1. Continue in this manner, increasing 1 st each end of every right side row and keeping these new sts from this point on worked in St st. At 16 (17½-19-20½-22)" from beginning measured on the increased edge, begin to dec 1 st each end every right-side row, matching pattern as for first half, until 3 sts remain. Bind off all sts.

Lower Rib: With smaller needles, pick up and k 74 (80-86-92-98) sts along edge. Work as follows beginning with wrong side row: Reverse St st on 2 sts,

*Cable on 4 sts, Reverse St st on 2 sts; rep from * across. Work as established for 2". Bind off all sts.

Back Yoke: With larger needles, pick up and k 80 (88-96-102-110) sts on upper edge. Work as follows beginning with wrong-side row: Reverse St st on 2 (3-4-4-2) sts. *Cable on 4 sts, Reverse St st on 2 sts; rep from *, end Cable on 4 sts, Reverse St st on 2 (3-4-4-2) sts. Work even for 2½". Next row, work on 26 (27-33-34-37) sts and leave on holder, work on next 28 (34-30-34-36) sts and leave on holder for back of neck, work to end of row and leave these sts on holder.

Front Yoke: Leaving center 5½ (6¾-6-7-7)" free for front of neck, work on both sides at the same time and pick up and k 26 (27-33-34-37) sts on each side using 2 separate skeins of yarn. Work in pattern to correspond to back yoke for 2½". Bind off all sts.

Neckband: Join shoulder seams using the knitted seam method. With circular needle, pick up and k 80 (92-84-92-96) sts around neck opening and work in k2, p2 rib for 1". Bind off all sts in rib.

Armhole Bands: Sew side seams, leaving an 8½ (9-9½-10-10½)" opening for armholes. With circular needle, pick up and k 88 (92-96-100-108) sts around opening. Work in k2, p2 rib for 1". Bind off all sts.

Finishing: With damp cloth and warm iron, block carefully into shape.

Blends of fibers can be tricky, but when successful they produce lovely fabrics like the one in this ramie-based vest. The construction is neat, too, and because casting-on is at a minimum, you can start knitting within seconds of picking up your needles.

FIBER

type and source: Raw Icelandic wool from Louise Heite.

characteristics: Icelandic fleece contains two distinct types of fibers: coarse ones 6-10" long and fine, well-crimped, short ones. This combination produces the characteristically lofty "Icelandic" yarn.

preparation: The wool was picked, scoured, teased, carded, pulled, and spun, then the yarn was dyed. We ended up with more weight lost between raw and finished states of this fiber than is usual, because a lot of volcanic ash tends to collect in the wool of true Icelandic sheep.

SPINNING TECHNIQUE: Supported long draw, with extra attention to amounts of twist.

DYEING

dye type and source: PRO acid dye from PRO Chemical in turquoise, blue, and violet.

process: Each of these dye colors was mixed into a 3% stock solution (3 tablespoons dye powder with 1 pint boiling

(continued)

A bulky, softly twisted yarn knits up quickly into a cozy pullover that's both practical and stylish.

Because we wanted to retain the loft in this fiber and keep the yarn soft, there's a minimum amount of twist. This makes it challenging for the spinner to get the right number of twists per inch.

We kept the yarn smooth so its texture wouldn't compete with the color pattern. The design concept is based on two colors with value (or dark/light) contrast. Our colors were lavender and a variegated purple/blue mix. We dyed the spun yarn, and the wool did not take the dye as intensely as we expected it to. Rachael had to use considerably more dye than she usually would for this quantity of fiber. The sweater could be worked in a solid color, with or without a textured stitch pattern. If you choose another stitch, be sure its gauge is the same as ours.

The resulting sweater is warm enough to be worn through a reasonable winter (we're talking Maine, so "reasonable" means pretty cold) if covered by a nylon shell to break the wind. We worked on circular needles, to eliminate side seams and breaks in the pattern. As a result, the armhole openings are cut instead of shaped in the knitting process. This can be unnerving, but once you've done it you'll like the results—both for the ease of knitting the pattern and for the way the finished sweater goes together.

Hélène wanted this sweater to be *comfortable* and stylish. Drop shoulders and a wide crew neck make for an easy fit. The shaped lower edge is higher in front, which is flattering to the hips, and lower in back, to keep out breezes. While the style is an obvious hit with younger sweater wearers, it's also practical for and pleasing to other recipients.

KNITTING INSTRUCTIONS

Instructions are for finished size 40". Changes for size 44" and 48" are in parentheses.

Materials: Louise Heite's Icelandic wool, spun to bulky weight: 16 (18½-20¼) ounces or 370 (430-470) yards each light shade (A) and dark shade (B). One each 24" size 9 and 11 circular needles or size to obtain correct gauge. One set each double-pointed and 16" circular needles in same sizes.

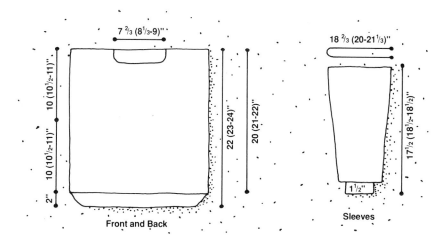

7 2/3 (8 1/3-9)"

10 (10 1/2-11)"

10 (10 1/2-11)"

2"

22 (23-24)"

20 (21-22)"

Front and Back

18 2/3 (20-21 1/3)"

17 1/2 (18 1/2-18 1/2)"

1 1/2"

Sleeves

Gauge: In St st and Color pattern with size 11 needle, 3 sts and 3.5 rows=1".

Stitches Used: *Stockinette stitch.*

Note: Back shirttail is done first, then sts are cast on for the front; body is then worked around in one piece to shoulders.

Back: With larger 24" circular needle and A, cast on 49 (55-61) sts. Work back and forth in St st following chart 1, inc 1 st each end every right-side row beginning on row 3 as indicated on chart until 59 (65-71) sts are obtained.

Front: Wrong side facing, with A, cast on 61 (67-73) sts at beginning of row, then turning work so that right side is facing you, work across 59 (65-71) sts from back—120 (132-144) sts. Place marker on needle for beginning of row and continue in pattern working around (k every row) until 18 (19-20)" from front cast-on row. Break yarn.

Shape Neck: Leave center front 19 (21-23) sts on holder. Attach yarn at right side of front neck and, working back and forth in St st, keeping Color pattern as established, dec 1 st at each neck edge every other row 2 times—97 (107-117) sts. Work even until 20 (21-22)" from front cast-on row. Next row, bind off 37 (41-45) sts. Leave next 23 (25-27) sts on holder for back of neck. Bind off rem sts.

Sleeves: With smaller double-pointed needles and A, cast on 26 (28-30) sts. Work around in k1, p1 rib for 1 1/2", inc 10 (12-10) sts evenly in last row—36 (40-40) sts. Place marker at beg of row. Then, with larger needles, work around, knitting every row following chart 2, and inc 1 st each side of marker every 1 1/2 (1 2/3-1 1/3)" 10 (10-12) times working new sts in Color pattern—56 (60-64) sts. Work even until 17 1/2 (18 1/2-18 1/2)" from beginning. Bind off all sts.

Armhole Openings: Find armhole placement evenly spaced on each side of body. Measure 10 (10 1/2-11)" from shoulder edges and place marker. With sewing machine and a fairly short stitch length, make a zigzag seam down to marker, double-stitch at that point, then stitch back up to shoulder seam, leaving approximately 1/4" between seams (see illustration). Carefully cut between seams without cutting thread.

water), then added to the two dyepots as follows:

#1, light lavender: 2 tsp. violet

#2, variegated: 6 tsp. each of turquoise, blue, and violet

The acid dye technique is described for sweater 2 (Novelty Yarn Pullover). To get a darker color we tried adding extra acid to the dyebath, but even with extra acetic acid, not all of this dye was absorbed by the wool.

YARN
weight: Bulky (3 stitches/inch).
yards per pound: 370.
number of plies: 2.
singles t.p.i.: 3.
plying t.p.i.: 2.

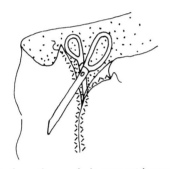

Reinforce the armhole area with two rows of machine stitching before you cut the fabric.

Neckband: Sew shoulders together. With smaller 16" needle and A, begin at left shoulder seam and pick up and k 7 sts on side of neck, work across 19 (21-23) sts from front holder, pick up and k 7 sts on side of neck, work across 23 (25-27) sts from back holder. Work around in k1, p1 rib on these 56 (60-64) sts for 1". Bind off all sts in rib.

Lower Edge Ribbing: Attach yarn at left side "seam." With smaller 24" circular needle and A, pick up and k 11 sts on rounded corner, pick up and k 49 (55-61) sts on edge of back, pick up and k 11 sts on rounded corner, pick up and k 61 (67-73) sts on edge of front. Work around in k1, p1 rib on these 132 (144-156) sts for 1". Bind off all sts in rib.

Finishing: Set in sleeves at armhole openings.

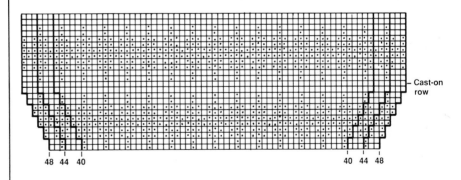

Key to color chart

☐ = A
☑ = B

Conclusion

Although this concludes our book, it is by no means the end! We could have kept going indefinitely—ideas were still bubbling forth. Each sweater inspired at least five other ideas. Many fibers were not included, simply because of lack of time and space. Countless techniques in spinning and a rainbow of colors are yet to be combined by knitters, spinners, and dyers.

To keep in touch with constant changes in the fiber industry—new fibers, old fibers in new preparations, new dyes and ways to apply familiar ones—contact suppliers and get on their mailing lists, and watch fiber magazines.

We hope this book gives you many useful ideas and spurs you on to create more innovative designs. We wrote this book to serve as a guide and inspiration for the many sweater designs which can be sparked by our imagination and yours!

Hélène and Rachael

Acknowledgments

Our sincere appreciation to the people who helped us present to you such a large number of designs in an amazingly brief period of time. Special thanks to the following:

For all their patient knitting, Susan Wills, Ona Moody, Carol Esterberg, Letty McDonough, Donna Flynn, and Casey Collins.

For their generous gifts of fibers: Brown Sheep, Euroflax, Fallbrook House, Louise Heite, Jones Sheep Farm, R. H. Lindsay, Moose Crossing, The Silk Tree, Silver Crown Farm, Straw Into Gold, Gerald H. Whitaker, Wilde Yarns, Wildhaere Farm, and Wildwood.

For their contribution of colorful dyes: Cerulean Blue, Ltd., W. Cushing and Company, PRO Chemical and Dye, and The Ruggery.

And a special thank you to Louët for kindly providing us with their S-10 spinning wheel.

One more person needs to be mentioned here: Patty Meyer, who introduced us to each other and started all this!

Fiber, dye, and equipment sources

The suppliers whose materials we used in preparing this book are listed below; several have detailed catalogs or newsletters, filled with helpful information. Most will provide samples of their wares. You can learn a lot by taking classes (through your local weaving/spinning shop or guild) and by trying different wheels and equipment.

Other sources can be located through the advertisements in such publications as *Spin·Off, Handwoven, Shuttle Spindle & Dyepot, Surface Design Journal, The Black Sheep Newsletter, Angora Quarterly*, and weaving and spinning guilds' newsletters. Of course, don't forget your local suppliers and sheep breeders—you'll notice we remembered ours!

FIBERS AND EQUIPMENT

Brown Sheep Company, Inc., Route 1, Mitchell, Nebraska 69357. (308) 635-2198
   Suppliers of commercially spun yarns (appropriate substitutes for some handspuns), as well as carded rovings for the handspinner.

Euroflax, Inc., P. O. Box 241, Rye, New York 10580. (914) 967-9342
   Suppliers of natural and dyed flax, in rovings and line fibers, as well as linen yarns.

Fallbrook House, R.D. 2, Box 17, Troy, Pennsylvania 16947. (717) 297-2498
   Suppliers of silk fibers in various forms, including caps and cocoons.

Louise Heite, P. O. Box 53, Camden, Delaware 19934. (302) 697-1789
   Importer of Icelandic fleece, yarn, and rovings.

Jones Sheep Farm, R.R. 2, Box 185, Peabody, Kansas 66866. (316) 983-2815
   Suppliers of fleece of many different breeds of sheep.

R. H. Lindsay, 393 "D" Street, Boston, Massachusetts 02210. (617) 268-4620

   Suppliers of wools and other fibers, raw, carded, and as tops.

Louët Sales, P.O. Box 70, Carleton Place, Ontario, Canada K7C 3P3. (613) 257-5793

   Suppliers of Louët spinning wheels and equipment.

Moose Crossing, Anne and Allen Gass, R.F.D. 1, Box 370, South Paris, Maine 04281. (207) 743-7656

   Breeders of registered natural-colored sheep for fine handspinning wool.

The Silk Tree, Box 78, Whonnock, British Columbia Canada V0M 1S0.

   Suppliers of luxury-quality yarns and handspinning fibers.

Silver Crown Farm, R.D. 3, Box 363, Chester, New Jersey 07930.

   Suppliers of rovings from a variety of breeds of sheep and of luxury fibers.

Straw Into Gold, 3006 San Pablo Avenue, Berkeley, California 94702. (415) 548-5247

   Suppliers of yarns, fibers, and spinning equipment.

Gerald H. Whitaker, Inc., P. O. Box 305, Niagara Falls, New York 14305.

   Wholesaler of yarns and handspinning fibers.

Wilde Yarns, 3737 Main Street, Philadelphia, Pennsylvania 19127. (215) 482-8800

   Suppliers of carded wool in natural and dyed colors.

Wildhaere Farm, P. O. Box 144, Limington, Maine 04049. (207) 637-2835

   Breeders of angora rabbits and suppliers of angora fiber and yarn.

Wildwood, R.R. 2, Box 388, Rte. 144, Westport Island, Maine 04578. (207) 882-7926
Suppliers of quality fibers and equipment for the handspinner.

DYES

Cerulean Blue, Ltd., P. O. Box 21168, Seattle, Washington 98111-3168. (206) 443-7744
Suppliers of many types of dyes, dye information, and dye equipment.

W. Cushing and Company, P. O. Box 351, Kennebunkport, Maine 04046. (207) 967-3711
Suppliers of Cushing's Perfection Dyes for cottons, silks, and wools, and the all-fiber type of dye.

PRO Chemical and Dye, Inc., P. O. Box 14, Somerset, Massachusetts 02726. (617) 676-3838
Suppliers of varied types of dyes, dye information, and dye equipment, as well as Synthrapol wetting and pre-scouring agent.

The Ruggery, 565 Cedar Swamp Road, Glen Head, New York 11545.
Suppliers of Craftsman's Dye for wool, which is an acid dye.

Bibliography

Some of these books may not be available at your local bookstore, weaving shop, or knitting supplier. If you have trouble locating them, try Schoolhouse Books, 6899 Cary Bluff, Pittsville, Wisconsin 54466, or Unicorn Books, 1304 Scott Street, Petaluma, California 94952.

Blumenthal, Betsy, and Kathryn Kreider. *Hands On Dyeing*. Loveland, Colorado: Interweave, 1988.

Don, Sarah. *The Art of Shetland Lace*. London: Bell and Hyman, 1980.

Fanderl, Lisl. *Bauerliches stricken + 2*. Rosenheim: Rosenheimer Verlagshaus, 1979.

Fannin, Allen. *Handspinning: Art and Technique*. New York: Van Nostrand Reinhold, 1970.

Fee, Jacqueline. *The Sweater Workshop*. Loveland, Colorado: Interweave, 1983.

Gottfridson, Ingvor and Ingrid. *The Swedish Mitten Book*. Asheville, North Carolina: Lark, 1984. Inspiration for patterns.

Harmony Guide to Knitting Stitches, vol. 1 and 2. Los Angeles: Lyric Books, 1988.

Horne, Beverly. *Fleece in Your Hands*. Loveland, Colorado: Interweave Press, 1979.

Knutson, Linda. *Synthetic Dyes for Natural Fibers*. Revised edition. Loveland, Colorado: Interweave, 1986.

Leszner, Eva Maria. *Handschule Mutzen schals farbig gestrickt*. Rosenheim: Rosenheimer Verlagshaus, 1980.

Lind, Vibeke. *Knitting in the Nordic Tradition*. Asheville, North Carolina: Lark, 1984.

Mon Tricot Knitting Dictionary. Paris: Mon Tricot, various dates (updated regularly).

Raven, Lee. *Hands On Spinning*. Loveland, Colorado: Interweave, 1987.

Ross, Mabel. *The Essentials of Handspinning*. Kinross, Scotland: Mabel Ross, 1980.

_____. *The Essentials of Yarn Design for the Handspinner*. Kinross, Scotland: Mabel Ross, 1983.

Spin·Off. Magazine published by Interweave Press, 306 N. Washington Avenue, Loveland, Colorado 80537.

Teal, Peter. *Hand Woolcombing and Spinning: A Guide to Worsteds from the Spinning Wheel.* Dorset, England: Blandford, 1976.

Walker, Barbara. *A Treasury of Knitting Patterns.* New York: Charles Scribner's Sons, 1968.

_____. *A Second Treasury of Knitting Patterns.* New York: Charles Scribner's Sons, 1970.

_____. *Charted Knitting Designs: A Third Treasury of Knitting Patterns.* New York: Charles Scribner's Sons, 1972.

Zimmermann, Elizabeth. *Elizabeth Zimmermann's Knitter's Almanac.* New York: Charles Scribner's Sons, 1974 (New York: Dover, 1981).

_____. *Knitting Without Tears.* New York: Charles Scribner's Sons, 1971.

_____. *Knitting Workshop.* Pittsville, Wisconsin: Schoolhouse Press, 1981.

INDEX

acid dye 17-18, 38, 56, 63, 64, 75, 78, 95, 105, 111, 115, 119, 129
all-fiber dye 17, 81, 99
angora 8, 25-26, 56, 60, 64, 69, 124

balanced yarn 14
blending fibers 11, 88, 115, 124
bulky weight yarn 1, 37, 69, 129

cables 38, 70, 111, 124; 4 stitch 53; 8 stitch 48; 16 stitch 92
camel 8, 75, 124
carding 11, 21, 27, 119
Corriedale fleece 69
Cotswold fleece 87
cotton 2, 8
crimp 6

draw 12-14
dyeing prodedure 19-20

equipment 21-23

fiber choice 6
fiber reactive dye 18, 90, 103
finishing yarn 15
Finn fleece 119
flax 43

garnetting 46-47
gauge 1, 16, 28-29

Icelandic fleece 129

knitting abbreviations 30-31
knitting techniques 31-32

Lanaset dye (see Telana dye)
length of fiber 6
light bulky weight yarn 1, 35, 46, 95, 112, 116
light worsted weight yarn 1, 56, 90, 99, 125
linen 8, 24, 43-44, 103
luster 7

Maine island fleece 51, 77, 124
measuring handspun yarn 15-16
Merino fleece 77, 99
mohair 8, 24, 69, 111, 124

Navajo plying 115
novelty yarns 25, 37

picking the fleece 10
plying 14, 24, 37
procion dye 18, 90, 104
pulling 12

quantity of yarn 8, 29-30

rainbow dyeing 95
ramie 8, 24, 124
Romney/Perendale fleece 95

safety with dyes 19
scouring 10, 46
sheep breeds 7
Shetland Island fleece 64, 77, 81
silk 8, 24, 56, 69, 75, 90, 103
singles 96
size of fiber (fine or coarse) 6
singles 14, 24

spinning oil 115
sport weight yarn 1, 60, 75-76, 81-82, 103, 119-120
stock solution of dye 19

teasing fiber 11
Telana dye 18, 51, 78, 87
twisted rib 111-113
two-ply 35, 37, 43, 46, 57, 60, 66, 69, 76, 82, 88, 90, 103, 106, 120, 125

three-ply 51-53, 54, 112, 115-117

variegated yarns 25

washing 10
weight of fiber 8, 29
Welsh Mountain fleece 105
wheel ratio 14
wheels 21
worsted weight yarn 1, 43, 54, 66, 81-82, 88, 106, 119-120